This book is part of the Victor FAMILY CONCERN SERIES, a multivolume library dealing with the major questions confronting Christian families today. Each book is accompanied by a Leader's Guide for group study and a Personal Involvement Workbook for individual enrichment. All are written in a readable practical style by qualified, practicing professionals. Authors of the series are:

Anthony Florio, Ph.D., premarriage, marriage, and family counselor, *Two to Get Ready* (premarital preparation);

Rex Johnson, assistant professor of Christian education, Talbot Seminary, active in pastoral counseling, *At Home with Sex* (sex education and marriage preparation in the family);

Harold Myra, publisher of *Christianity Today, Love Notes to Jeanette* (sexuality and fulfillment in marriage);

J. Allan Petersen, speaker at Family Affair Seminars, *Conquering Family Stress* (facing family crises);

Nancy Potts, marriage and family counselor, *Loneliness: Living Between the Times* (dealing with personal loneliness);

Wayne Rickerson, family pastor, Beaverton Christian Church, Beaverton, Oregon and director of Creative Home Teaching Seminars, *Family Fun and Togetherness* (family togetherness activities);

Barbara Sroka, served on research and writing committees with Chicago's Circle Church and is active with their single adults, *One Is a Whole Number* (singles and the church);

James Thomason, assistant pastor at Calvary Baptist Church, Detroit, *Common Sense about Your Family Dollars* (family finances);

Ted Ward, Ph.D., professor and director of Values Development Education program at Michigan State University, *Values Begin at Home* (value development in the family);

H. Norman Wright, assistant professor of psychology at Biola College and marriage, family, and child counselor, *The Family that Listens* (parent-child communication).

Consulting editor for the series is J. Allan Petersen, president of Family Concern Inc.

Family Fun and Togetherness

Wayne Rickerson

While this book is designed for the reader's personal enjoyment and profit, it is also intended for group study. A Leader's Guide with Victor Multiuse Transparency Masters and a Personal Involvement Workbook are available from your local Christian bookstore or from the publisher at $2.95 each.

VICTOR BOOKS

a division of SP Publications, Inc., Wheaton, Illinois
Offices also in Fullerton, California • Whitby, Ontario, Canada • London, England

Scripture quotations are from the *New American Standard* Bible,
© 1960, 1962, 1963, 1968, 1971, 1972, 1973 by the Lockman
Foundation, La Habra, California.

Recommended Dewey Decimal Number: 248.4
  Suggested Subject Headings: FAMILY; HOME; DOMESTIC RELATIONS

Library of Congress Catalog Card Number: 79-63539
ISBN: 0-88207-641-8

VICTOR BOOKS
A division of SP Publications, Inc.
P.O. 1825 • Wheaton, Illinois 60187

Contents

Preface   9

1   Family Fun and Togetherness—
      Who Needs It?   13

2   Family Night—
      Best Night of the Week   25

3   Togetherness Around the Table   43

4   Trips, Vacations, and
      Other Great Adventures   53

5   Celebrations of Special and
      Not-so-special Occasions   65

6   Family Activities That Say "I Care"   75

7   Three Games to Make and Play   85

8   Simple Games for Family Fun   97

9   Homemade Holidays   109

10   Togetherness Through Work
      and Hobbies   120

11   Togetherness Through Reading   124

12   How to Plan for Family
      Fun and Togetherness   129

Foreword

Wayne Rickerson is minister of Family Life and Christian Education at Beaverton Christian Church in Beaverton, Oregon. He is a speaking consultant with Family Concern, a consulting editor for *Family Life Today* magazine, and the author of four other books on the family. He is the founding director of Creative Home Teaching Seminars, an organization that helps equip parents to teach Christian values at home.

If I could start my family again, one thing would be changed. I would play more with my three boys, and cultivate more family sharing experiences. By sharing good times a family builds cohesiveness and unity. They learn to enjoy each other and compensate for each other's weaknesses. The play of children is something of a rehearsal for life, and parents who share these times of play will have a great opportunity to teach their children how to live.

Wayne Rickerson has built on this concept to establish a ministry to families in his local church and through creative home teaching seminars. In *Family Fun and Togetherness* he shows us how the family is drawn together through shared fun, and how conscientious Christian parents can use these fun times to teach important biblical truth. The ideas he suggests have been tested in his own family and with a variety of families in churches where he has ministered. No one family will be able to use every idea in this treasure chest, but I can hardly imagine a Christian family who will not welcome and use many with great profit.

The Family Concern Series is an encyclopedia of practical family information prepared in response to the needs of contemporary families. It enables the church, with its built-in structures for education and enrichment, to meet these needs with a thorough and long-term plan. Pastors and church professionals will find in the books many valuable resources. They focus on the needs of singles, marrieds, parents, and the family.

God uses people more than books to change people and this series helps people work together on their family needs. Each book can be used in a group study for mutual learning, encouragement, and support.

A Leader's Guide provides 13 study plans for adults in Sunday Schools, seminars, workshops, conferences, and retreats—complete with learning activities and visual aids.

A Personal Involvement Workbook enables each individual to get maximum benefit from the study whether alone, as a couple, or in a group. Worksheets and activity instructions are included. The Guide to Curriculum Subjects works as an index to the most important topics and where they are mentioned in each book in the series. It is a road map that will help you find quickly the information you need.

A special word of appreciation goes to Norman Stolpe. As Family Concern's editorial director he served as series editor for this project. His vision and relationship with the various authors enabled the concept to take form in reality. His hard work brought this series from planning to completion.

Victor Books and Family Concern have shared this vision and have cooperatively developed this comprehensive family ministry resource for individuals and churches. I trust God will deeply enrich your life and family through it.

J. ALLAN PETERSEN
Family Concern, Wheaton, Illinois

Preface

Yesterday my wife Janet and I bought a little plaque with brightly colored houses inscribed, "Now is the Time to Live Tomorrow's Memories." At the conclusion of the evening meal we showed it to our three children, Heidi, Liesl, and Bridget. Our eighth-grade daughter Heidi's face brightened as she said, "That's us Dad. That plaque was made for us."

I couldn't agree more. The things we are doing today with our families are warm memories that last a lifetime.

Memory ideas—things to do as a family that you can add to your album of family memories is what this book is all about. Reading together, trips, games, discussions, celebrations, and working together, are essential if you want to build real family togetherness. Why? Because shared activity produces communication and communication is the lifeblood of the family.

Of the many family activity ideas in this book, some you will like, others will not interest you. This is because your family is unique. Perhaps you are a one-parent family. This would influence which activities you would choose.

Some of you have very young children, while others have older children. We have three girls. Some of you may have all boys. Others may have just one child. There are some homes where grandparents or others live with the nuclear family.

Be selective with the type of activities you feel your family will need and enjoy. Many of the ideas in this book can be adapted to your special situation.

And go easy on yourself. Some activities you try will work and others won't. When an activity falls flat, don't feel that something must be wrong with you if it doesn't work with your family. Just smile and congratulate yourself for eliminating one more thing that doesn't work with your family.

The important thing is to commit yourself to building

family togetherness in your home. And, when you feel the pressures that can separate you from that precious family time, remember, "Now is the time to live tomorow's memories." Tomorrow is too late.

GUIDE TO CURRICULUM SUBJECTS

	Wright—Communication THE FAMILY THAT LISTENS	Ward—Values Development VALUES BEGIN AT HOME	Thomason—Finances COMMON SENSE ABOUT YOUR FAMILY DOLLARS	Sroka—Singleness ONE IS A WHOLE NUMBER	Rickerson—Fun & Togetherness FAMILY FUN AND TOGETHERNESS	Potts—Loneliness LONELINESS: LIVING BETWEEN THE TIMES	Petersen—Crises CONQUERING FAMILY STRESS	Myra—Intimacy in Marriage LOVE NOTES TO JEANETTE	Johnson—Sex Education AT HOME WITH SEX	Florio—Premarriage TWO TO GET READY
adolescent children	*	*					*		*	
birth control								*	*	*
child development	*	*			*				*	
child discipline	*	*								
child communication	*	*			*		*		*	
church-family		*		*			*			
dating				*					*	*
death						*	*			
divorce				*		*	*	*		
emotions	*			*		*	*	*		*
engagement							*	*	*	*
finances			*				*			
friendship				*		*		*		
goals		*		*		*				*
leisure					*				*	
loneliness				*		*				

1
Family Fun and Togetherness— Who Needs It?

When the Rickerson family moved to Beaverton, Oregon, we went through the typical stresses and hassles of most long moves. Can you remember your first night in a new house? What a drain! We unloaded the U-Haul truck, set up the beds, and put some of the furniture in place.

About 9:00 P.M. I groaned and dropped onto the couch in the living room. A few minutes later Liesl, our 10-year-old daughter, came in. I noticed she was acting a little strangely. She paced back and forth, stared at the furniture and sighed a couple of times. "Dad," she finally said, "this doesn't seem like our house." "It will soon," I assured her. "It takes time to feel at home in a new house."

Liesl started to pace again. "Now this part of the room," she continued, pointing to our old rocking chair, table, and lamp, "seems like home. Let's have a fire."

"A what?" I asked in a shocked voice. "Liesl, it's probably still 75 degrees in here." She gave me a look that said, "You don't understand, Dad."

Then it hit me. I had missed the whole point of her actions. We were uprooted from family and friends. This was a strange place. Were things going to be the same in our family? Liesl was feeling the insecurity that most of us feel when we move.

"Could we do something with the whole family, Dad?" Liesl's persistence finally paid off. "Would you like to have the family sing a few songs, read a psalm from the Bible and talk for a while?" I asked.

Liesl's face beamed. "That would be great." A very tired family spent a few minutes together in an activity that said, "Things have not changed—we're still a together family."

Emotional Security Needs

Who needs family fun and togetherness? Liesl did. Our togetherness as a family gave Liesl the courage to face her new life in Beaverton. It was a real source of security. Not only Liesl, but *all children* need a feeling of family unity. Doing things together is one of the keys to happiness in a family, and to the adjustment of children. As parents, we sometimes get so wrapped up in the business of being adult that we forget that family time is essential to the emotional security of children.

Children in our society no longer have the security of living in one place with aunts, uncles, cousins, and grandparents near by. Life is different. We move. Many times our roots are not deep enough even to make lasting friendships. In these days the children need the security of family unity more than ever before.

Parents Magazine asked psychologist David Elkind, "What do you see as a major need in families today?" His answer, "Contemporary parents should be more concerned about the emotional needs of their children and the quality of time they spend with them" ("What Young Children Need Most in a Changing Society," July 1977, p. 58).

Not only psychologists and other students of the family see the need for family time. Children do also.

"Look at it from the viewpoint of 1,500 school children who were asked the question, 'What makes a happy family?' The most frequent answer was 'doing things together.' It's not so much what we do *for* our children that makes fun at home as what we do *with* them" (*How to Keep Your Family Together and Still Have Fun,* Marion Leah Jacobsen [Grand Rapids: Zondervan Publishing House] 1969, p. 19).

Doing things together is what this book is all about. Shared activities are a kind of adhesive that keeps the family together. The brand of "glue" you use is not important. Families are different and the activities you share should be what your family enjoys. This book is full of many different kinds of family activity suggestions. The idea is for you to choose the things your family will enjoy.

The Bond family has built great togetherness around competitive sports. The three Bond boys are the primary participants, but the entire family focuses on the athletic activities.

The Maples family from Seattle, Washington has a different kind of "family glue"—a family night each week and activities around the dinner table. I found out how enthusiastic their children were about their family times one evening at church after I finished showing some slides of families doing things together. Two of the Maples' teenage girls came bubbling up, "Those are the kinds of things we've done," one commented. "Some of the best times I can remember in our family were the nights when we read the *Little House* series. Mom would put a red checked tablecloth on the table and light a kerosene lantern. Then we would read a chapter or two. Family nights and our times around the dinner table were our best times."

The Maples are a military family. They have moved often, but their special kind of "family glue" has held well. Now two of the girls are in college, but they say they "just can't wait to get home" for some more warm times of conversation around the dinner table.

Bernard J. White recalls an old-fashioned kind of "family glue" that held his family together. "My most vivid memory, and one that has influenced me tremendously, is of family togetherness. Both parents and children were simply expected to share the work load and then share the fun.

"Sundays were always special days. After church and breakfast we would often pile into the 1939 Chevy—how vividly I remember that historic car, since it was our family car until 1952—for a Sunday drive. Living in the Pacific Northwest, we had many vistas beckoning us: mountains, beaches, the old swimming hole of the little Washougal River. We usually packed a picnic lunch and enjoyed a leisurely day of running, hiking, or swimming" *(What They Did Right,* Virginia Hearn, ed. [Wheaton: Tyndale House Publishers] 1974, p. 204).

Hebrew Family Unity
Such family togetherness usually produces children who are deeply committed to the Lord and who possess an extra measure of self-confidence. This should not surprise us, for God has always intended that values be communicated through the family in an atmosphere of family love. Godly values are not passed on from parents to children in a vacuum. They grow in an atmosphere of healthy interaction and are based on good relationships between parents and children. The only way that relationships are built within a family is by time spent together. Of course, not all relationship-building time is family time. It is very important for parents to spend time with each child alone. But time with the entire family present is a great way to build relationships. It is through "togetherness" activities—working, playing and sharing together that we really get to know one another.

God's plan for families is one that produces unity. Think of the Old Testament Hebrew family. Virtually everything happened within the family circle, as the members shared together in work, and the parents taught godly values to their children. The social and recreational life of the family centered in the home, though sometimes including the extended family.

All of these shared activities in which the early Hebrew family participated provided a family bond that held the family together during the worst of conditions. Have you ever wondered about the homes from which Daniel, Shadrach,

Meshach, and Abednego came? What kind of special family relationships would give four young men the courage to stand against the heathen government which held them captive? It was due to their societal structure—centered in family and tribe, and based on the revealed Law and Covenant of Jehovah—that the values of the Hebrews were passed on from generation to generation.

The importance of the Hebrew family unity in passing on values is told us by the psalmist:

> Listen, O my people, to my instruction; incline your ears to the words of my mouth. I will open my mouth in a parable; I will utter dark sayings of old, which we have heard and known, and our fathers have told us. We will not conceal them from their children, but tell to the generation to come the praises of the Lord, and His strength and His wondrous works that He has done. For He established a testimony in Jacob, and appointed a law in Israel, which He commanded our fathers, that they should teach them to their children; that the generation to come might know, even the children yet to be born, that they may arise and tell them to their children, that they should put their confidence in God, and not forget the works of God, but keep His commandments (Ps. 78:1-7, NASB).

North American Families

You might be thinking, "That was thousands of years ago in an agrarian society. The family is no longer an economic unit. Fathers work outside the home. Parents no longer have to teach children at home, since so many things enrich their lives outside the home."

It is true that life is more complicated for families today. I am thankful for the opportunities my children have to learn, and that I do not have to teach them all they need to know to be successful. Nevertheless, I can't overlook this basic principle: *Families still learn to love and understand one another by spending time together—by sharing in activities.* Values are still passed on from generation to generation as parents take the time to build relationships with their children as individuals and within the family circle.

One thing is certain: It is not easy to find time to build the kind of family unity we have been talking about. It seems as though society in general obstructs the family as it tries to walk the way of togetherness. Think of the competition: school activities, television, fathers commuting or working out of town for extended periods of time, church and youth programs, sports, enrichment activities for the children—and I'm sure you can add some items to this list yourself.

Many North American families are succumbing to the pressure and spend very little time together. I find that many don't even have a sense of "familyness." Awhile ago a family moved in across the street. They have a girl the same age as our youngest, Bridget. She simply cannot understand that our family does things together. When she knocks at the door after dinner or is asked to go home because we are going to have family time, she always asks, "Why?" Janet and I have both tried to explain, but the little girl has never experienced family togetherness and cannot understand.

This is not an isolated case. People have reacted in similar ways in other neighborhoods in which we have lived. My experience in working with many families has taught me that an alarming number of parents do not see the importance of spending time together as families. Many are in the business of doing things *for* their children but not *with* them.

The Portland *Oregonian* recently surveyed Oregon high school seniors about their opinions and experiences. That survey was compared to a similar survey given to Oregon high school seniors in 1948. One particular item stood out. Today's Oregon youth spend much less time together with their families than did the teenagers of 1948. In 1948, 82 percent of the respondents said their families engaged in leisure activities as a group. Last year, only 24.5 percent of the youth said they did things together as a family "often." Another 48 percent said they participated in family activities "sometimes" while 19 percent said they seldom had such activities and another 3.5 percent said such activities "never" happened (*Governor's Commission on Youth: High School Opinion and Attitude Survey 1976, The Oregonian,* January 2, 1977, Rod Patterson).

Lack of family time in homes is a potentially explosive situation that can lead to family disaster, if the trend toward doing things away from the family is not reversed. The consequences of parents not spending time with their children are distressing. Urie Bronfenbrenner, Professor of Human Development and Family Studies at Cornell University, has spent much of his life studying what effect lack of family time has upon children. In his minority report to the White House Conference on Children he wrote,

But it is not only children from disadvantaged families who show signs of progressive neglect. For example, a survey by this writer of changes in child-rearing practices in the United States over a 25-year period reveals a decrease, especially in recent years, in all spheres of interaction between parent and child. A similar conclusion is indicated by data from cross-cultural studies comparing American parents with those from Western and Eastern Europe. Moreover, as parents and other adults move out of the lives of children, the vacuum is filled by the age-segregated peer group. Recently, my colleagues and I completed a study showing that, at every age and grade level, children today show a greater dependence on their peers than they did a decade ago. Our evidence indicates that susceptibility to group influence is higher among children from homes in which one or both parents are frequently absent. In addition, "peer-oriented" youngsters describe their parents as less affectionate and less fair in discipline. Attachment to age-mates appears to be influenced more by a lack of attention and concern at home than by any positive attraction of the peer group itself" *(Report to the President, White House Conference on Children.* [Washington, D.C.: U.S. Government Printing Office] 1971, p. 253).

From his research in numerous countries, Dr. Bronfenbrenner has found that American parents rate next to last in the amount of time they spend with their children *(Two Worlds of Childhood,* Urie Bronfenbrenner. [New York: Pocket Books,] 1973, p. 116). Yet many parents wonder why they cannot communicate with their children. They are outraged by the children's rejection of their values.

But what about Christian families? Certainly they spend more time together than non-Christians? I have not observed this to be true. In fact, Christian families often add many church programs to their already-cluttered schedules. Most of these are segregated by ages, and leave even less time together for the family.

The Fight for Family Time

You may say, "You don't understand our situation." I'm sure I do not. Just as you would have difficulty understanding ours. We all have our "impossible" situations that keep us from family time.

I'm not denying the difficulty of making time to spend with the family. Our family certainly finds it hard. The older the children become, the more complicated their schedules are. Almost every week Janet and I have to reevaluate our calendar, taking a hard look at the things we are doing. It is so easy to overextend ourselves with "worthwhile and interesting" activities. Janet and I regularly have to eliminate some involvements that get in the way of the family.

We are responsible for our own schedules and we can find time for family activities if we really want to. It depends on what we value. If we value the family then we will sacrifice less important activities. If we do not value the family then it will indeed be "impossible" to find family time.

Motivation to have an adequate amount of family time must come from the parents' belief that it is essential to family life. Our society does not make it easy. But God's Word says that we are not to "be conformed to this world, but be transformed by the renewing of your mind, that you may prove what the will of God is" (Rom. 12:2). As parents, we need to "renew" our minds and give the family the high priority that God desires.

The Christian Family

I believe most Christian parents have an earnest desire to see their children grow up to be successful Christian persons. They give many years of their lives to their children, investing time, prayer, thought, energy, money, and love. I believe most Christian parents feel that their greatest reward in life is to see this investment pay off in happy, Christian children.

There is another, more immediate reward, however. That is the loving spirit that permeates a home where there is family fun and togetherness. I am *not* saying that family time is a cure-all for all family problems, or that the family will be free of hassles if they spend a lot of time together. We have problems in our family, as I'm sure you do in yours. Family togetherness, however, creates a climate of closeness that makes family members think, "We will work this out because we care. We are a family." This closeness lasts even after the children are grown and the family is no longer physically together. However, if the family has had little closeness when they were together, they will have even less when the children are gone. How often have you heard parents say, "Our children never come to see us. They just don't seem to care. I don't understand why they can't take the time to visit."

The reason is obvious. There never was much fun and togetherness in the home while the children were growing up, and now there is no magnet to draw them back when they are adults and have families of their own. Actually, the children have learned their lesson well. In their growing-up years within the home, the parents did not communicate that togetherness was important. Now that the children are gone, and the parents feel a need for the children to want to come back home, the children are living out what they learned at home—"Our family is really not that important."

Children raised in homes where family fun and togetherness was valued by the parents want to return to the family setting. Edith Schaeffer writes beautifully about her family's togetherness and how, now that the family is far apart, everyone looks forward to the annual reunion. Why does this family excitedly look forward to the family reunion invitations that are sent out each Christmas? Because of the diligent work the Schaeffers have always put into their family. They are simply receiving the rewards of family togetherness. If you have read *Hidden Art* or *What is a Family?* by Edith Schaeffer, then you know how this family worked, planned, and sacrificed for family fun and togetherness. Now that the children are grown and have families of their own, the highlight of the year is the family reunion—returning to relive some of the old memories and build some new ones.

It is not family perfection that creates closeness in families. If that was the case, then the Rickerson family would be in trouble, for we have our share of problems. There are no perfect persons, and no perfect families. Our imperfections, however, give us an opportunity to help each other grow.

Edith Schaeffer ties imperfection closely to growing together as a family:

This family reunion did not come about because of perfect people, nor because of having had perfect relationships every moment of every day, nor because of having always made the right decisions, nor because of calm perfect dispositions and easy-to-live-with characters. There has been a long succession of mistakes, and sins, forgiveness asked for and given, troubles and feelings of hopelessness, discouragement to the point of wanting to give up, hard lessons learned, and a fresh learning from each other. The older ones have learned from the younger, as well as the opposite way around *(What Is a Family?* Edith Schaeffer. [Old Tappan, N.J.: Fleming H. Revell] 1975, p. 27).

The Bible says, "Tribulation brings about perseverance, and perseverance, proven character; and proven character, hope; and hope does not disappoint, because the love of God has been poured out within our hearts through the Holy Spirit who was given to us" (Rom. 5:3-5).

We don't have to be perfect. In the midst of all our imperfections we can have happy growing families. The essential ingredients are parents who are willing to make the family a high priority. When this happens, the children will also feel that the family is very important. The reactions from our children are what make the work of building family togetherness all worthwhile. Just a few days ago, Bridget spoke to me about her new friend that just moved in a few houses away. "Dad," Bridget said, "you know Kelly doesn't know what family nights are. She doesn't know anything about special times with dads, and she doesn't know Jesus. *She doesn't know anything!"*

I just grinned and thought, "It's all worthwhile."

2
Family Night—
Best Night of the Week

"My Daddy went hunting last week and missed family night," six-year-old Jeremy complained to a member of our church in an irritated voice. "And family night is the best night of the week."

The Powells had started regular family nights only two months before, but for Jeremy it was already the best night of the week. Most children I know agree. Family nights are incredibly popular with children.

What is this family night that is so exciting to children? A family night is a once-a-week time when the entire family is together for activities that grow from the parents' understanding of God's Word. The whole family participates—has fun together—and that is what makes it so exciting for children.

I'm convinced there is not a better way to have family fun and togetherness than to start regular family nights. Our family has been doing this for four years, and it is hard for us to imagine family life without it.

I'll always remember the day Janet and I were reminded of just how important family nights are to our children. Our first family night of the new year fell on January 1. We had been up late on New Year's Eve. New Year's Day had been full of activities—going to the zoo in the morning and a trip to a Swiss candy-maker in the afternoon. My wife and I were really beat so we contrived to just "overlook" family night for once and see if the children would do the same.

They didn't. Around 5:00 P.M. Heidi said, "Dad, you haven't forgotten about family night, have you?"

"No," I groaned.

"You don't sound very enthusiastic, Dad. You act like you don't even have anything planned."

I gave Heidi my little spiel about how tired we were and how many "family things" we had already done that day. She listened patiently and then said, "All right, Dad, I see you don't want to do anything, so I'll plan family night."

She did, and the whole family had fun, including a weary Mom and Dad.

Come to a Family Night

Since it's difficult to explain how a family night works, how about joining us in our family room to see for yourself?

A cozy fire crackles in the fireplace. Janet, the girls, and I are sitting on the floor around the fire. "Do I get to do my special thing first?" asks Bridget. "Not yet, Honey," I reply, "Heidi is leading the first activity." Bridget frowns and mutters something under her breath.

Heidi starts the family night by announcing the topic, which is "Choosing Friends." Next she says that we are going to play a game called "Who am I?" "I will read some statements about a Bible character," she explains, "and you try to guess who it is. When you think you know, raise your hand."

Heidi reads several of the clues and finally Liesl's hand shoots up. "I know, I know," she shouts. "It's Jonathan."

Heidi asks me to read 1 Samuel 20. She then asks the family what qualities of friendship they noticed in the story of David and Jonathan. We discuss this for several minutes.

Liesl takes over and leads a discussion on choosing friends. She has us do such things as "Tell something about your best friend, describe the qualities you look for in a friend, and tell what qualities we should possess to be a good friend to others."

Now it's Bridget's turn (by this time she has asked at least a dozen times when her turn starts). She sings a song that she has made up about friends. She tries to teach it to the rest of the family, but she changes the words each time so we get a little mixed up.

"What's for dessert, Mom?" Heidi asks.

"Hold it," I break in. "Let's have a circle of prayer first and then we will find out what Mom has for us." We pray, especially thanking God for our friends and asking God to help us always to choose good friends.

Janet unveils the dessert for the evening. A shout of approval goes up from the starved Rickerson children. "Warm chocolate chip cookies and milk. Great!" Mom has scored again with a popular family night dessert. We finish off one or two dozen cookies and the girls are off to bed.

Now with the children in bed, let's evaluate what happened. First, did you notice that there was a warm, informal atmosphere? This is important. Make your family nights as informal and relaxing as possible.

And did you notice that everyone participated? This was not "Mom and Dad Lecture Night." That afternoon I had made the assignments for family night. I used a family night plan from *Family Life Today,* a magazine that contains four family night plans each month. I made sure each family member had something specific to do. And I made sure that they understood their assignments.

The material you use is important. But you will have to adapt it to the age level and interest of your family. Besides *Family Life Today,* there are other good resources that you can use. Two books, *Happiness Is a Family Time Together,* and *Happiness Is a Family Walk with God,* by Lois Bock and Miji Working, (Revell) have good family night plans. Elva Anson's *How to Keep the Family that Prays Together from Falling Apart* (Moody) has many good ideas for family nights. I have written a book called *Good Times for Your*

Family (Regal) which has over 100 family activities, many of which can be used on family night.

You do not have to feel tied to printed material, however. Create some of your own family nights. Ask your children for suggestions. Use lots of variety. Summer is especially good for doing things in God's great outdoors. The important thing is that you commit yourself to one night a week that is labeled "family only." Don't let anything interfere with that commitment.

Now, to help you get started, I would like to suggest that you try family nights for the next four weeks. Read through the following family night plans. Each plan contains more ideas than you will want to use on a single family night. Don't try to use all the activities in each plan. *Select only the ones that you feel your family will enjoy and ignore the others.* Remember, pass around the responsibilities. Make sure everyone in the family has something to do. Have fun, and don't forget that special dessert. I suspect that at the end of the four weeks, family night will be a permanent part of your family life.

Family Night One
What Makes a House a Home?

Goal: The goal of this family night is to help family members appreciate your home and to encourage them to express this appreciation by doing at least one thing to make your home a happier place to live.

For Parents: We rarely take time as a family to think of the many beautiful ways in which God helps us make our house a home. Some day our children will reflect upon their home and relive memories that we are building now. What will they think of? Will they have warm memories from which to draw strength in later years?

God, the Master Builder, wants to use us, His carpenters, to build beautiful Christian homes. Family nights can be a useful tool for building memories in the home. Use this family night to think together on "What Makes a House a Home?"

1. The Home Happening. Mom and Dad should start this family night by describing the house or houses in which they spent their childhood. Describe not only what the house looked like but also what made those houses happy homes to live in.

Give each family member a house cut-out as described below and have him write under the doors and windows what he feels makes a house a home.

Prepare these house cut-outs in advance for your family. Use one sheet of construction paper for each. Cut out a large house (approximately 6" x 8") similar to the one shown in Figure 1. Cut the two windows and one door so that they will open. Trace the house you have just cut out on a plain piece

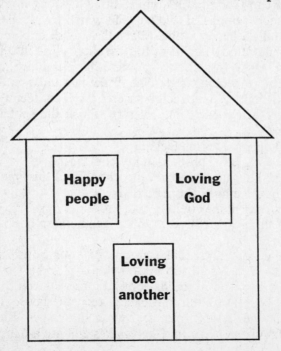

of white typing paper, then glue the paper to the back of the construction paper house. Now each window and the door has paper behind it to write on.

Have each person, in turn, open the windows and door on his or her house and write or draw what makes a house a home.

Discuss how loving God, loving one another, doing things together, being considerate of each other, and sharing God's Word together, help make a house a home.

2. Who builds the home? Read Psalm 127 and discuss the following questions.

Who builds the home?

In what ways does God build our home?

How can God use parents to build a happy home?

How can God use children to build a happy home?

Have each person list two ways in which he can be used of God to build a happy home. Share these with one another.

Challenge family members to turn their ideas into personal goals that will help make the home a happier place to live.

3. Finish the sentences. The following open-ended sentences will help family members express their feelings about your home. Have each one, in turn, finish the sentences out loud.

My home makes me feel . . .

The thing I like best about my home is . . .

When I am away from home, the thing I miss most is . . .

My best memory about home is . . .

I wish our home could be more . . .

One thing I could do to make our home a happier place to live is . . .

4. The grand tour. Take a tour of your house. Go into every room and have each person think of some way he can help make it a happy room. Some things that could be done are: help keep the bathroom clean, keep the bedroom clean, pick up in the living room, and wash the dishes. Remember that the family working together makes a house a happy home.

5. *Treasure hunt.* Cut out five three-inch-high houses on which to write the clues to the treasure. Plant the clues in various rooms of the house. Have the final clue lead to the kitchen. The treasure should be a special snack that you have ready for your family.

6. *For families with teens.* This activity will help you get better acquainted as you think about one another and your home. Every home has a "family personality"—a composite of the values and interests of the occupants. However, if one person were to design a home only for himself, it would reflect his personality.

Have each person choose another family member for whom to design a home. This home should reflect that person's interests and personality. You may either sketch the house or write a short story describing what this person's house would be like. Be specific. What kind of furniture would he prefer? What colors would he use? What hobbies or interests would be in evidence?

When this project is done, ask the person for whom you planned the house how close it is to being accurate. Then as a family discuss the following:

In what ways does our home reflect the personalities of the various family members?

What are some things that make our house a home?

What do you like best about our home?

What changes will you make in your own home?

How can our home be improved?

Have each person think of one thing he will do to make your home a happier place to live.

7. *For families with young children.* With a little adapting, the Home Happening, Grand Tour, and Treasure Hunt activities will work well with young children.

Another activity you might enjoy is to play house with your little children. Select some dress-up clothes. Let the little ones be the mother and father and you the children. Have this activity lead you into a discussion of the following questions:

What makes a happy home?

How does loving God help make a happy home?

How does loving one another help make a happy home?

How does helping Mother and Father help make a happy home?

How does obeying help make a happy home?

How does doing things together help make a happy home?

Have each child think of one thing he will do to help make your home happy.

Family Night Two
Caring For Personal Possessions

Goal: This family night is to help family members become more sensitive to others' feelings about personal possessions and to develop some guidelines for respecting the rights of others in the family.

For Parents: Lack of respect for personal property within the home is a problem in many families. One reason for this recurring problem is that children have difficulty identifying with the feelings of others. This is caused, in part, by their limited conceptual development. They have problems putting themselves in the place of others.

This family night is designed to help your children become more sensitive toward other people's feelings about personal possessions. Select the activities you think your children will appreciate.

1. My most prized possession. Have each person conceal his most prized personal possession and bring it to the family circle. If the possession is too large to hide, it may be left in its place until later in the activity.

Family members must guess what everyone's personal possession is by asking each person not more than 10 yes-or-no questions about that possession. Go around the family circle with each person asking one question until the possession has been discovered or the 10 questions have been asked. The person being questioned must then show his possession and tell why he chose it.

Use this procedure until all family members have shown their prized possessions.

Discuss: How do you feel when someone mistreats your possessions? What other personal possessions should be respected? (mail, clothes, jewelry, etc.)

2. Unscramble the verse. Each house below contains a word of a very special Scripture verse: "Treat others as you want them to treat you" (Luke 6:31, LB). Unscramble each word and place the words in proper order to discover the verse. See Figure 2.

Discuss: How can this verse help us respect other family members' personal possessions? What changes must we make in our actions?

Now give each person five minutes (more or less, depending on the ages of your children) to study the verse. When the verse has been memorized, say the first word of the verse and go around the family circle with each person adding a word until it is completed. If someone misses a word, start over.

3. Picture the verse. Give everyone a piece of paper and crayons or marking pens and have him draw a picture that illustrates the principle of Luke 6:31. This could be a picture of a family member showing respect for another's personal possessions. Show and discuss these pictures when all family members have completed their pictures.

4. Role play. Have two of your children role play the following situations: One child is sitting in his room studying. Another child barges into the room, takes something without asking and walks out. Tell your children to act out the roles in their own way. They are free to use whatever gestures or conversation they feel is appropriate.

Stop the role play before a solution is reached and discuss what happened. Who was at fault? What rights were violated? How did the other person respond? What could have prevented the unhappy situation?

Now have your children role play the same situation again, this time being considerate for one another's personal rights and possessions. Discuss the difference between attitudes represented by the role plays.

5. *The Untouchables.* Have each family member make a list of personal possessions he wishes others would not touch without permission. Next have everyone take a new piece of paper and write each family member's name on it. Beside each name he should list that person's "untouchables." Each person should keep his list to remind him of the importance of respecting other family members' personal possessions.

6. *Personal possessions and sharing.* There is always the danger of becoming selfish with our personal possessions. We need to remember that all we have comes from God. There is a delicate balance between protecting personal possessions and sharing with others. To help clarify this balance discuss the following questions:

a. When should we be willing to share our personal possessions?

b. Are there times when we should not share our personal possessions?

c. Read Luke 6:31 and Matthew 22:39. What principles do these verses contain that can help us know when and what to share?

7. *Personal possession policy.* On the basis of the Scriptures you have read and your discussion, formulate a one-sentence policy for your family about personal possesions.

Have each family member write this policy on an index card and keep it in his room as a guide to solving the sticky problems concerning personal possessions.

8. *For families with teens:* Adolescents have very strong feelings about their rights to privacy. Use "the untouchables" activity to open up communication on this topic. Have a free, open discussion of your feelings about personal possessions and come to some kind of consensus on a policy for personal possession rights.

9. *For families with young children:* Have a show-and-tell with your children. Each person, including parents, should bring his favorite personal possession and show it to the rest of the family. Because young children will probably bring toys, you might want to take a few minutes to play with them.

Tell the following story about Danny's broken plane. It will help your children understand the importance of respecting other people's personal belongings.

10. *Story of Danny's broken plane.* Danny is five years old and is in kindergarten. Danny's mother had a beautiful glass figurine of a boy and his dog. Danny's mother always said, "You can look at it, Danny, but never pick it up. If you dropped it, it would break."

Danny wanted to pick it up just once. One day he decided, "I'll be very careful and just pick it up a little." Danny picked up the figurine. He dropped it, and it broke.

Danny's mother was very sad that her figurine was broken. "Danny," she said, "you disobeyed when you picked up my doll. Now it is broken and cannot be fixed."

Danny wished he had not touched it. But it was too late. It was already broken.

Later that day, Danny's friend Adam came over to play. "That's a pretty plane, Danny," Adam said. "Can I fly it?"

"No, it's only to look at," replied Danny. But when Danny left the room to get some cookies, Adam tried to fly the plane. And it broke. Danny cried because that was a special plane. His father had given it to him on his last birthday. Now it was ruined.

That evening Danny told his father what happened. "Danny," his father said, "I know you are very sad that the plane is broken. That's just how your mother feels about her broken figurine. People always feel sad when something very special is broken."

"They sure do," Danny replied. "I'm going to leave other people's things alone from now on."

Discuss this story with your children. 1. Why was Danny's mother sad? 2. How did Danny feel when Adam broke his plane? 3. How would you have felt? 4. Can you think of a rule about touching other people's things? (Always ask before you touch.)

You might want to give your child a small present. Tell him that the present is his, and no one is to touch it unless they ask him first.

Family Night Three
Caring For Family Possessions

Goal: During this family night each family member should come to understand the value of family possessions and feel his responsibility to help care for them.

For Parents: In most homes the care of family possessions is a continual problem. Parents end up maintaining most of them. Children need to be taught early in their lives that family possessions are the responsibility of the entire family.

The activities in this family night are designed to help you communicate this value to your children. Choose the activities that you feel your family will enjoy.

1. Family possessions: Start this family time by having members tell what their favorite family possession is and why (such things as car, television, dog, house, etc.).

Next give each member a pencil and piece of paper. Have him draw a stick-figure picture of the family at the top. Under the picture on the left side of the paper, have him list in a column all the family possessions he can think of in the next five minutes. To the right of each family possession have everyone list the person or persons who are responsible for taking care of that item.

Share your lists with one another and discuss the following:
What is a family possession?

How do you feel when your favorite family possession is misused?

What responsibility does each family member have in the care of these possessions?

What happens when someone does not care properly for a family possession?

Which of our family possessions need better care? In what ways could the family take better care of them?

2. *Possession problems.* Colossians 3:12-17 gives a list of qualities that Christians should possess. Read this Scripture aloud and have the family decide on two qualities that, if lived out, would help everyone to be more responsible with family possessions.

The following are four problems about family possessions that occur in many homes. Read each of these and discuss what the person or persons mentioned in the case studies would do differently if he were "living out" the two qualities from Colossians.

a. Roger has a steady girl friend and likes to use the family car on dates. Many times Roger's father finds the gas tank empty when he gets ready to go to work in the morning. When it is time to clean the car on Saturday, Roger says he can't help because of his studies and part-time job.

b. Cindy, age 8, likes to listen to the family records, but lately she has not been putting them away properly and several scratches have been noticed on them.

c. Dishes are a big hassle at the Johnsons. Not only do the Johnson children complain bitterly about having to do the dishes, but they also usually just leave glasses and plates wherever they happen to be eating.

d. The Rollins family has several family games they all enjoy playing. They each take turns putting the games away after they have been used. But Chris is usually quite careless and just "throws" the games into their boxes. The games are beginning to look terrible and the rest of the family is upset.

3. Family possession project. Decide on a family possession that needs some tender loving care. Use the rest of your family night working on that project. You might wash the car, clean the yard, wash the windows, clean up the camping equipment, etc.

4. A personal commitment to care for family possessions. Have each family member finish the following open-ended sentences:

"A family possession I sometimes misuse is_____.
In the future I will be more responsible by _____
_____."

Signed, _____

5. Money and possessions. God expects the Christian family to use its money wisely. Proper care of family possessions is a good way to save money. Tell family members that because of the money the family will save as a result of their commitment to care for family possessions, you are going to treat them to something of their choice (within reason, of course).

6. For families with teens. In many homes the family car is a special problem. Discuss the following questions and adopt some type of mutually acceptable guideline for car use.

• What are the priorities for car use?

• Who is responsible for upkeep of the car? What things must be taken care of?

• Who pays for damage done to the car?

• What should the procedure be for asking for permission to use the car?

• What limitations should be imposed if the car is misused?

7. For families with young children. Even young children can learn that they are responsible to care for family possessions.

Prepare four sheets of paper. From magazines, cut pictures of a mother, father, children, and family. Paste one of these at the top of each piece of paper.

Next, cut out about 15 pictures of various family and personal possessions. For instance, some pictures you might cut out are a television set, house, car, doll, perfume, toy, stove, dog, game, etc.

Place the four papers and the 15 pictures in front of your children on a table. Tell them to look at the pictures, decide to whom they belong, and then paste them on the appropriate sheet of paper. For example, they would paste the picture of the perfume on the paper with the picture of the mother. The television would be pasted on the paper with the picture of the family at the top.

When this project is completed, discuss the pictures. Talk about the fact that some things are personal possessions and others are family possessions.

Ask why the car is a family possession. (Because the whole family uses it.) Talk about some ways that the whole family can keep the car clean. Ask what happens when family members leave papers, toys, and other items in the car. Use this procedure to discuss each of the pictures.

Choose a family possession that you can work on together, such as cleaning the car or the yard. Let your young children help you work on this project. As you work, discuss the importance of each family member helping to care for family possessions.

Praise your young children for their help. Have an extra special treat for the young workers.

Family Night Four
Listening Is Fun

Goal: This family evening is designed to increase communication in the family as members sharpen their listening skills.

For Parents: It is estimated that we hear only about 25 percent of what is said. If that is so, then there must be something wrong with the way we listen!

Family communication is extremely important and listening is a crucial part of communication.

As parents, we need to be examples of good listeners. Do we hear our children through, even when we disagree? Are we sensitive enough to look behind their words to what they really mean?

During this family night, your family should increase its sensitivity toward one another as they learn to listen in love.

Choose the activities that fit your needs and interests. Are you listening?

1. Gossip. Write on a slip of paper a sentence about any subject. Whisper the sentence into the ear of another family member. He whispers the same sentence, exactly as he hears it, into the ear of the person next to him, who in turn repeats it to the next person. After everyone has heard the sentence, the last person repeats it aloud. Compare what he says with the original sentence.

Was the sentence given by the last person different from the original? What does that teach about listening?

2. Concentrate. Tell family members that you are going to play a listening game that takes concentration. Have one person stand in the center of the room. He walks up to another family member, touches a part of his own body, and says, "This is my leg" (or foot, finger, head, etc.) as he points to a part *different* than the one he has named, such as an eye. The person he is standing before must point to whatever has been named, in the preceding case, the leg, and identify the part pointed to by the leader saying, for example, "This is my eye," before the leader counts to 10.

If he fails the listening test before the count of 10 he replaces the one in the center.

3. Listen, listen, listen. Read Proverbs 18:13. What does this teach about listening? Have each person give an example of how this verse is true.

4. Your third ear. Do you have a third ear? If not, you can start growing one right now. Develop a sensitivity to what a person is really saying. A third ear hears beyond words and tries to understand underlying thoughts and feelings. Discuss:

- How do you feel when you know someone is really not listening?
- Do you sometimes feel a need for someone to listen to you in an understanding way?
- How do you think someone else feels when he knows you are not really listening?
- Name three ways you could be a more understanding listener.

5. *The longest minute in the world.* Let each family member, in turn, talk for one minute. After a family member has completed his one-minute ordeal, the rest of the family should discuss what they think he said. Then he shares with the family what he meant to say. What were the differences? What does this say about listening? Let each family member have a turn.

6. *For families with teens. Parent-teen listening test.* Parents and teens can take the following test. After completing it, share the results. Discuss how listening in the home can be improved.

- Do you wait until *parent/teen* is through talking before having your say?
- Do you respect *parent/teen* opinions?
- When *parent/teen* talks, do you pretend you're listening when you're not?
- When *parent/teen* talks, do you let your preconceived ideas screen out what he is saying?
- When *parent/teen* talks do you listen or are you thinking about what you are going to say when he is finished?

7. *For families with young children:* Young children will become good listeners if their parents set a good example by listening attentively to what they and other people have to say. Make sure that you give them a good example to follow.

Another way to help young children become good listeners is to have them memorize short lines or stories. Read the lines or stories to your child in short sections and have him repeat it. He will soon have it memorized. Help your child learn the following poem:

God gave me two ears and I can hear. (Point to ear.)

I can hear my daddy. (Point to Father.)

I can hear my mommy. (Point to Mother.)

I can hear my brothers and sisters. (Point to brothers and sisters.)

When they speak I listen. (Cup hands around ears.)

Thank You, God, for ears. (Fold hands and look up.)

3
Togetherness
Around the Table

If I were an enemy of the United States and had been told by my government to destroy the American family, I would start by sabotaging the family meal. I would deluge family members with so many separate activities that they would rarely be able to sit down to eat together. If they did happen to have a meal together, I would make a diligent effort to cause this time to be a real hassle: arguments, tenseness, and each family member wanting to "get on to his own thing" as soon as possible.

Why would I attack the family meal? Because in most cultures throughout history, eating together has been the major activity that draws the family together. It has been the heart of family communication. When you weaken this part of family living, you damage the entire family structure, and the family then becomes vulnerable to other attacks.

"Wait a minute," you say. "Aren't you putting too much emphasis on a single part of family living? The family meal is important but it seems like you're overdoing it a bit."

I don't think so. Consider, for example, the Japanese families that were in American relocation centers during World War II. In these internment camps the Japanese family went through its greatest crisis, with significant breakdown

43

of their family units. Why? Because the only time the family was together was at night. Even then they were all crammed into one room regardless of age or sex. But when morning came everyone was on his own. *Even at meals children did not sit with their parents.*

Daisuke Kitagawa, in his book *Issei and Nisei—The Internment Years,* sees this disruption of the family table as the major factor that contributed to the breakdown of the Japanese family:

"The family table, under normal circumstances is an institution around which the life of the family as a unit is centered. It is where children 'eat and drink' their parents' love and care for them, as materially symbolized in the meals earned by the father and prepared by the mother. Even in the completely secularized family, the family table is a sacrament of parental love for children and of the instrinsic unity and solidarity of the family. This was the element completely missing from life in the relocation center. . . .

"The loss of the family table and family kitchen was not simply a loss of opportunity to teach table manners to growing children, but a forceful symbol of the breakdown of that human institution which transmits moral and spiritual values from one generation to another. Man, indeed, does not live by bread alone" *(Issei and Nisei—The Internment Years,* Daisuke Kitagawa. [New York: Seabury] 1964, p. 86).

I feel that families in America are facing a similar breakdown in togetherness around the dinner table. Just as devastatingly as in relocation centers, we are allowing the great institution of the family meal to become less and less important.

American Eating Habits
Dr. Paul A. Fine, psychological consultant to several food companies, gave some surprising statistics about American family eating habits during a symposium on nutrition sponsored by the American Medical Association.

Dr. Fine pointed out several myths, one of which is that "Americans eat breakfast and dinner together as a family, drawing spiritual as well as nutritional sustenance from the shared ritual" ("Family Eating Study Yields Food for Thought," *Today's Child*, Vol. 22, March 1974, p. 1).

Dr. Fine's survey revealed that families tend to sit down to dinner together no more than three times a week and often less frequently. The dining rite is generally completed within 20 minutes. Three out of four families do not breakfast together; many skip breakfast entirely.

Add the fact that one out of three food dollars is spent on eating out and it is plain to see that the family table and kitchen is no longer what it once was.

The harsh reality is that families who do not value the importance of eating together are headed for problems. We saw such problems develop in a family with whom we attended seminary. I recall my wife exclaiming in disbelief, "Wayne, do you know that the Rogers don't even have a table on which to eat. They just use TV trays and spread themselves throughout the apartment."

The little on-campus duplexes in which we lived were small but we could not imagine anyone not having a table. Even then, their children were having severe problems. Some time later, the family was torn apart by divorce.

The importance of the family meal is awesome. Sharing a meal with others creates a closeness that is tangible. I believe that God in His great family plan saw meals to be a source not only of physical strength but also of spiritual and emotional strength. Meals are a focal point of many Scriptures. It is significant that Jesus chose the Passover meal as one of His last major activities with His disciples before He died. Jesus had a purpose in this. He wanted His disciples, and all future Christians, to continue to have intimate fellowship with Him and each other on a regular basis. It is through this shared meal that the family of God remembers Jesus' death.

If the family can be weakened by the loss of togetherness

at the table, then the opposite is also true. By using the great potential of eating together as a family, parents can build family strength and solidarity.

Corrie ten Boom found such strength around the oval table in her home while she was growing up.

"Can a piece of furniture be important? The oval table in our dining room was the gathering place for hopes and dreams, the listening place for prayers and petitions, and the loving place for joy and laughter. . . .

"Conversations around the dinner table were lively because we all had stories or experiences we wanted to share. I believe that the great enjoyment of a family eating together is having this time when each person can be heard.

"Father had a special talent in directing our talks so that no one would feel left out. We loved to tell personal stories, but were taught to laugh at ourselves, not to make fun of others" (In My Father's House, Corrie ten Boom. [Old Tappan, NJ: Fleming H. Revell Co.] 1976, pp. 61-62).

Corrie has rich memories of the "oval table" because someone saw its great potential for growth. Her father determined to make eating together a focal point of family life, and God rewarded his effort by giving his children great strength.

I recently heard of another father who decided that time around the table should have high priority. Paul Hunter, a young pastor in a little country church in Oregon, recently told me, "My Dad really used our times around the table effectively. He was a busy pastor but the breakfast and dinner hour were sacred. He allowed nothing to interfere. At this time, we shared the news of the day, talked about important things, argued, discussed, and read a portion of Scripture. This is my warmest memory of growing up."

An interesting sidelight to the Hunter story is that Paul moved to Oregon to be close to his father who pastors a nearby church. Why? "Because," Paul told me, "I want to continue to learn from my father. He has so much to offer a young pastor like myself."

Paul claims that "Even now when we spend the holidays with my parents, we linger at the table relishing each moment we spend together."

Meals as Family Times

I believe any family can make their times around the table the greatest times of all. How? By understanding what happens when the family gathers to eat, by developing a few skills, and through an honest commitment to make this time the core of their family life.

What happens when the family gathers around the table? What makes this time such an effective tool in building family unity?

1. The evening meal in most homes is the one time of day that has the potential to hold families together for interaction over an extended portion of time. Day after day, year after year, a family can spend an hour together at this time of day if they really want to. This adds up to a lot of consistent family time over a period of years. By the time the children leave home, this consistent interaction will have had a lasting effect on them.

Of course, this will never happen unless Mom and Dad agree that togetherness around the table is a priority. The entire family will have to make an effort to be present for meals, and then not hurry off to individual activities when mealtime is over.

2. The table is a personality clinic. Think of the many times personalities have been evaluated around your table. Have you ever heard comments such as "He always takes more than his share" or "Do you always have to interrupt?" or "Can't you be serious about anything?" The entire family tends to evaluate each other's personalities on a regular basis. Done with wisdom and kindness, this personality evaluation can be a great help in molding characters.

Our family personality clinic was in session just a few nights ago. "You ought to see the two new girls in my Core class,"

Heidi, our seventh-grade daughter, commented. "They are really gross."

She went on to describe in detail what she felt made these girls unattractive. I was disappointed. You can imagine some of the conversation that followed. We talked about inward beauty versus outward beauty, how it feels to be new in a school, the attributes of kindness, and sensitivity towards others. It started as a lecture from Dad, I'll admit, but quickly turned into a family discussion. We all, in one way or another, evaluated Heidi's personality.

3. *The table is a time to share things of interest.* Heidi, smarting from the effects of the family reprimand for her attitude toward the new girls, diverted attention by introducing something of current interest to her.

"We had a lady from Syria in our social studies class today," she said. "She was really interesting. I'd like to tell you why there are not many thieves in Syria but I think I'd better wait until we've finished eating."

Janet looked up quickly with that "Don't you dare!" look on her face and said, "If it's very gory I think that would be wise, Heidi."

"I bet I know why they don't steal," blurted out Liesl after everyone had finished eating. "It's because they cut off their heads in public."

"Liesl!" Heidi fumed. "Let me tell about it. You do that all the time; try to tell someone else's story." (Another personality evaluation.)

"That right, Liesl," I intervened. "Let Heidi tell her own story."

"They don't cut off their heads," Heidi continued. "But they do cut off their right hand the first time they steal, and their left hand the second. Then they start on their feet."

As we discussed the merits of this type of punishment, the after-dinner conversation moved to the death of John the Baptist, and then on to more lighthearted subjects.

Usually each child will have something of interest he will

want to share at the table. This will be especially true if you encourage the sharing of information and experiences, and give each person an equal chance to talk. This is a good opportunity for your children to practice oral expression and the difficult art of listening.

4. *The table is a good time to clarify Christian values.* Christian values are things God thinks are important. God has given these in His Word and they comprise our standard for Christlike living.

Honesty is a Christian value that was clarified at our dinnertime recently. While my wife, Janet, was looking at jewelry rings in a department store, she saw an Avon spoon ring on the counter. Since Avon is sold direct and not in stores she immediately knew that someone had left it.

"I wondered if I should keep it or turn it in," Janet shared with the family. "I thought, if I turn it in, the saleslady will probably keep it. On the other hand, if I keep it the person who lost it might return and ask if it has been found. I decided to turn it in," Janet explained. "I felt it was the only really honest thing to do."

"But what happens if the lady doesn't come back for it, Mom?" Liesl asked. "Then it should be yours. But how are you going to get it back?"

"You could just go in and ask for it. They would think you were the one who lost it," someone else offered.

"But would that be completely honest?" I asked. "Wouldn't it be better for Mom just to phone the store and ask to have the ring returned to her if no one claims it?" The family agreed that this was the most open and honest thing to do.

Notice the way in which this Christian value was clarified. Mom admitted that she was tempted not to turn it in. Why should the store get it? However, she did the honest thing and turned it in. But how should she get it back if it was not claimed? Again honesty was clarified. A less than honest way of reclaiming it was suggested but revoked. Total honesty was the decision—after values were clarified.

Some might question if an item of low monetary value is worth all this discussion. We think it is. The decision to be honest is not based on the worth of an item but on the character of God and our identification with Him in Christ. If the principle is learned in smaller things, it will carry over to the larger.

5. *The table is a clearing house for information.* Everyone is together. Information can be shared and family schedules reviewed. Things that need to be done can be discussed and announcements made. For the evening meal, I like to save exciting bits of information that involve the entire family, especially about places we are going or unexpected surprises.

6. *The table is a good place for group discussions.* Of course, many of these things we have already talked about involve group discussion. But this is so important I want to mention it separately. Much of the discussion is informal, but occasionally it is good to plan family discussions. For example, the other night I brought up a topic for us to talk about. "What should be done about our car problem? Should we sell both older cars and buy a new one? Should we save until we have enough money to pay cash? Should we buy a compact or a medium-sized car?"

7. *The table is important because it is a symbol of the unity of the family and the mother's and father's love for the children.* Each time your family sits down together to eat it is a visual reminder—an object lesson—of these two things. Providing the food is an act of love. Preparing the food is an act of love. The family sharing food and talking together is a forceful sign of unity.

Improving the Quality of Time You Spend at the Table
Anything as important as time around the table deserves our best effort. The atmosphere should be positive—bright and cheerful. A well-decorated table will help. Candles and placemats add a lot to a dinnertime atmosphere.

Form some rules, such as "Each person washed and ready

for dinner at a certain time," or "No one asks to leave the table until Mother or Father says it's time to go."

Take advantage of informal situations at mealtime. Many times things that happen naturally are the best. But it is also good to intersperse these with planned tabletime activities. I would like to suggest a few that can help liven up those important times around your table. Try some that you feel your family will enjoy.

1. Plan for variety in the way you eat. Eat in different places. For example, during the winter you might want to have a picnic in front of the fireplace. Fix picnic type foods. Your children will love this.

• Plan a progressive dinner in your own house. Have various rooms host your dinner courses. Perhaps main course in the kitchen, salad in the family room, appetizers, dessert, etc., could be in your children's bedrooms. You could give them the responsibility of getting their rooms ready and serving a certain course.

• Have a smorgasbord. Fix some extra novelty type dishes and have family members file by the table and fill their plates.

• Have you ever thought of being a carhop for a meal? (If you're a mother you probably feel like one quite often.) Your children will never forget this meal. Prepare written menus and give them to family members. Take orders and deliver in carhop style. Dad will need to help too.

• Draw for food favorites. Prepare slips of paper with meat, dessert, salad, bread, drink, and surprise written on them. Have family members draw these slips. Then make a trip to the store and let each person buy for the evening meal what is written on his slip. (This will take some time and patience—works well on a family night.)

2. Show and tell. This is good to use with younger children. After dinner let each one go to his room and bring out something special to show and tell. Or, if the object is large, family members can go to where the special object is.

3. Reading together. After the meal, read aloud from a

book. This is such a great activity that I have devoted an entire chapter to it in this book.

4. *Joke night*. Children love silly jokes. Give each person a chance to tell his favorites.

5. *Discussion leader of the day*. Once a week appoint a family member to lead a family discussion. They should choose a topic they feel will interest the entire family.

6. *Question box*. This is one we have really enjoyed. Have the family write questions or topics they would like to discuss. Fold the papers and put them in a can or box. Periodically, have a child draw one out, and then discuss it as a family.

7. *Read from the Bible*. After dinner have someone read a portion of Scripture or a Bible story. You may want to discuss what you have read.

8. *Centerpiece creations*. Let your children take turns making a centerpiece for the table. They can use candles, favorite rocks, or other nature materials. Our children often do this when it is their turn to set the table.

9. *Whopper night*. Have one night when family members can make up outlandish stories. You can have fun laughing at these incredible episodes.

10. *Family Request*. Have family members pick a number between 1 and 20. The one who comes closest to the number you selected may make a special request of anyone else in the family. This request may be to sing a special number, run around the house twice, clean off the table, stand on your head or any other reasonable request.

"Better is a dish of vegetables where love is than a fattened ox and hatred with it." This proverb is a reminder that eating together and love go well when shared. Plan a steady diet of love to serve at your table and you will satisfy the emotional appetite of your family.

4

Trips, Vacations, and Other Great Adventures

Trips and vacations are not always equally enjoyable for every member of the family. I was reminded of this when we returned from a wonderful day in the snowy mountains.

After we arrived home, weary from all the physical activity, there was the usual mountain of clothes, food items and other things that needed to be put away. The children were faced with Saturday night baths.

"This is totally unfair," complained Janet. "The family enjoys a day out, but look who gets stuck with the work. You wonder why I am not very enthused when we take a trip? I feel like never taking another one."

I guess most mothers feel this way at times, and it's easy to see why. Let's face it, the situation is unfair. Why should Mom be stuck with the majority of the preparation and cleanup? The entire family should be sensitive to Mom's need for help and pitch in voluntarily, but that doesn't seem to be the way it works.

Try This Trip Tip

Let me suggest a solution to this dilemma, not as someone who has got it all together in this area, but as one who is trying hard to grow in this difficult aspect of family life.

Husbands and wives should always communicate and plan together the details of a trip or vacation. It should not be the wife's responsibility to nag her husband into a planning time. In fact, I feel it is the husband's responsibility to initiate a planning time with his wife. Why? Because God's Word says that the husband is the spiritual leader and head of the home (Eph. 5:21-33; 1 Cor. 11:3). The head gives direction, and there is no doubt that this area of family life needs some direction! This is a practical way for a man to show spiritual leadership within his home.

What can the husband do? He can set aside a time to plan, well in advance of the trip or vacation. He can ask his wife to make a list of things that will have to be done (1) before the trip, (2) during the trip, (3) and after the trip. Sit down together and discuss these tasks. Actually plan on paper how the responsibilities can be divided up. Maybe Dad could be responsible for purchasing and preparing the food. This would be quite a break for Mom. If they are old enough, the children can pack their own suitcases. Jobs can be assigned each family member during the trip. For example, on day one: Dad cooks, Jill will do all meal cleanup, Johnny will be responsible for tidying up the trailer or cabin.

Consider together what needs to be done when you arrive home. Obviously there will be a mountain of wash, things to be put away, the car to be cleaned, etc.

The times when we aggressively tackle these jobs as a family, things seem to go well. When everyone goes his own direction, we are headed for a family hassle. Again, planning is the key. Prepare the family ahead of time so each one will know what his responsibility will be. The family working together in this manner can save Mom hours of work the next day, and she will feel that the family cares about her needs.

Planning with your entire family is important. Remember, people cooperate better in things they help plan. Here is a procedure you could follow on a family night or some other appropriate time to plan your vacation.

1. Discuss possible vacation spots. Decide who will write the Chamber of Commerce in places that might interest you as vacation spots. Libraries also have information, as do travel clubs.

2. When you have enough information, make a family decision on where you will go. Make your plans in detail. Discuss the things you will do. Assign responsibilities for some of the tasks associated with your vacation. If possible make a copy of all plans for each family member. This will eliminate the typical excuses such as "I forgot" or "I don't remember having been assigned that job."

3. Commit your trip or vacation to the Lord. Read 1 Corinthians 10:31 together as a family. Discuss how you can do everything to the glory of God on this vacation. Be specific. Write suggestions on a piece of paper and place it with your other vacation material. Plan some spiritual enrichment activities for your trip. Have a special vacation family night. Take along one good Christian book to read aloud (like one of the *Chronicles of Narnia* by C. S. Lewis or Paul White's *Jungle Doctor*). How about making a project of learning some Bible verses—you could do this while traveling in the car. Pick out one of the shorter books of the Bible to read while on your vacation.

How to Prevent Car Trouble

Now I'm not talking about mechanical problems. This is much more complex. I'm referring to the problems that occur inside your car on a long (and sometimes short) trip.

"Don't touch me." "Susie's taking up too much room." "Quit making that noise. You're driving me crazy." "When will we be there?" These are all famous vacation quotations. I'm sure you could add some that are distinctive to your family. But they all have one thing in common. These problems cause "car trouble" and can turn what is supposed to be a great time into a nightmare.

One thing is for sure—we will never eliminate this kind of

problem completely, not as long as children are children and parents are parents. But we can do some things to significantly reduce friction on trips.

Try to see a long day in a car from a child's point of view. First, you would see only tree tops and tops of buildings. Did you ever stop to think that cars are made for adults, not children? A child, especially eight and under, cannot really see out of the normal car window. What he does see is UP—buildings, trees, and things that fly. Is it any wonder that kids poke one another or pester Mom and Dad?

We found something that helped solve this problem. We bought Cosco (TM) car seats for our children. These plastic seats are placed on the regular car seat. They elevate the children to where they can see out of a window. On each side there is a slit through which a seat belt can fit. Once our children started sitting in these chairs our "car trouble" was reduced greatly.

Notice I mentioned seat belts. I believe strongly in the use of these safety devices. As Christian parents I feel we need to do all we can to help preserve these gifts that God has entrusted to us. Besides, when children wear seat belts, it keeps them in one place. How many problems occur in your car because the children are moving around?

Another reason for many "car problems" is that our children sense that a different set of rules apply while traveling. We let our children get by with much more than they would at home because it is not convenient to discipline them while driving. Knowing this, children test their limits, which in turn tests the parents' sanity.

I have a suggestion which I do not always follow myself (and when I don't, I pay dearly). Cover your traveling ground rules with your family thoroughly before you leave; maybe even list the rules on an index card and tape it someplace in the car. Then follow through consistently on these rules, especially the first day. You'll be amazed at how much more pleasant your trip will be.

Be sure to take plenty of breaks on your trip. Some dads I know must think they're at the Indy 500—too many pit stops will lose the race. The whole family can use a 10-minute break every 2 hours. Have everyone get out of the car. Play tag for a few minutes. Get lots of physical activity and you will be much more relaxed and rested while in the car.

Things to Do That Prevent "Car Trouble"
There are many things that families can do together and individually while traveling. I'd like to share with you a variety of activities we have found helpful. Mark those you feel your children will enjoy and try them on your next trip.

1. Seat Bag. If your family is like ours, after three hours in the car the back seat looks like a junkyard. All these neat little activities we bring along for the children end up thrown on the floor. By the second day of the trip we can hardly see the children in the backseat because of the clutter. And clutter always seems to cause tension on a trip.

Janet decided to tackle this problem by making a seat bag as shown in Figure 3.

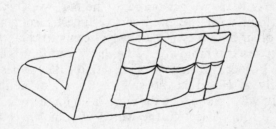

You will notice that this bag stretches across the back of the front seat so the children can reach it easily. The string that keeps it erect ties under the front driver's seat and passenger seat. The compartments can be made different sizes to hold the various activity materials for your children. You could have compartments for the crayons, scissors, paper dolls, games, books, or whatever you decided to take along. You might even want to label the compartments so the children can put things back in place when finished.

2. *Cassette Fun*. This is our children's favorite travel activity. We take along our cassette recorder, extra batteries, and blank tapes. We also include some tapes of songs and stories. This occupies the children for hours. Sometimes we use the cassette recorder for a quiet time—listening to songs or stories. Other times, the girls have hilarious fun recording little dramas, and a wild assortment of other unintelligible sounds that delight them when played back.

3. *Read a book*. "The time goes so much faster when we read," commented Heidi last fall on our return trip from Grandpa and Grandma's. I had just finished reading a chapter from one of the books in the *Chronicles of Narnia* series by C. S. Lewis. Books are a permanent part of our travel time activity list. Try this and see if the time doesn't fly for your family as well.

4. *Sing together*. Recently as we were returning home from the mountains with another family, things began getting a little hectic in the car. Bridget, our wiggly one, finally said, "Sometimes when we get bored in the car, we sing." It is not unusual for one of the children to suggest a song time when tired of other activities. This always seems to relax the family and make the trip more enjoyable. Now, our family is not very musical. In fact, we sing so off-key that many times we laugh at ourselves. But that doesn't dampen our enthusiasm— especially when riding in the car. You might want to make up a little songbook with the words of some of your favorite songs.

5. *Post card puzzles*. When you stop for a break let the children buy some post cards for their friends. Have each child write a message to a friend or relative, then cut the post card into puzzle-type pieces. Have the children place the post cards in an envelope and mail them. This project can be done while riding in the car.

6. Where am I? Someone in the family thinks of a location and then says, "Where am I?" The rest of the family, in turn, try to guess where that person is. The answer to each question must be Yes or No. After an appropriate amount of time, the person who is It must reveal his location if not guessed. Give each family member an opportunity to be It.

7. Zoo for you. Children love this game. Each family member "collects" animals for his zoo. For example, when he sees a dog, cat, sheep, cow, etc., he claims that animal for his own. At the end of a specified number of miles or time the person with most animals in his zoo wins.

8. Guess what I saw. This is similar to the game of 20 Questions. One person chooses something he has seen on the trip. The rest of the family, in turn, asks a maximum of 20 questions in an effort to identify what he saw. All questions must be answered with a Yes or No.

9. Add a word. Another word game that is popular with most children is "add a word." A family member starts this game by saying a word, for example, "dog." The next family member must say another word that starts with the last letter of the word just given. In this case that person would have to say a word that begins with "g," the last letter of dog. To make this game more difficult for older children you can choose categories. If you choose the category of "Bible persons," then all words must be names of Bible persons. Other categories such as cities, animals and food can be used.

10. Premonitions. This is a mental fantasy game. Each family member describes in detail something he feels the family will see within the next two hours. Then sit back and have lots of fun waiting to see whose "premonition" comes true.

11. License plate baseball. Appoint a scorekeeper. Have this person list all family members' names on a piece of paper. The first player takes the first license plate of the car that you pass or that passes you. If you are on a freeway with many cars, you might want to designate the first red car that passes you by as the "baseball" car. Every zero in that license plate is worth one run. If it is an out-of-state (or province) license it is worth an additional two runs. For example, an Arizona license plate (that is, if you are not in Arizona) with the number ABJ 0210 would be worth four runs (two for the two zeros and two for the out-of-state license). The next person on the list is now "up to bat" and gets the next designated license place. An inning is over when each family member has recorded his license plate. This goes on until seven or nine innings have been completed. Add up the scores and you have the winner.

12. Bowling license plate game. This is a special game for those who like to bowl and have older children. Draw up a bowling type score card. Appoint one family member to keep score. Use the same procedure as in the preceding baseball game to determine which car qualifies as the "bowling license plate" car. The first player then takes the first license plate that qualifies. The scoring is as follows:

If the license number starts with a zero it counts as a strike.

If it does not start with a zero, the first three numbers are considered as the first ball rolled. If the three add up to 10, it is counted as a strike.

If the first three numbers do not add up (any combination) to 10, then all other numbers in the license are considered. If a combination of any of these adds up to 10, it is counted as a spare.

If no combination totals 10, then any two numbers may be added that do not exceed 10 and are used as the pin count for the frame.

The first frame is over when everyone has had a turn. Ten frames are bowled and the scores are added to see who is the winner.

13. License plate bingo. Have each family member make two columns on a piece of paper. At the head of one column write State (or Province) and at the head of the other the number *4*. The first person to spot an out-of-state car must say the name of the state and "Bingo." He then lists that state in the column labeled states. If he can also give the capital of that state he places a *C* beside the name of the state.

Score one point for the person who first spots a number *4* on a license plate. An out-of-state license plate receives two points. If the person also is able to name the capital of that state he receives a bonus of two points. The first person who scores 30 points wins the game.

14. I spy. One person in the family is asked to name an object such as a barn, horse, tractor, stream, squirrel, etc. Family members watch closely to see who can be the first to "spy" the object. When a person sees the object he calls out, "I spy." That person then gets to name an object and the same procedure is followed.

15. Paper dolls. For the younger children, especially girls, a box of paper dolls can bring hours of enjoyment. It is best to have these cut out before the trip starts.

16. Activity books. If you have older children, take along some puzzle books. There are many crossword puzzle books and "hidden word" books that are educational as well as fun.

17. My very own travel fun book is a well-done activity book based on the Bible. This is a reasonably-priced book available in many Christian bookstores or it may be ordered from Warner Press.

Check your local bookstores and magazine stands. Many times they have useful travel booklets and magazines.

18. My own travel story book. Simply cut some regular-sized typing paper in half and staple it together in book fashion. Give this to your children and tell them it will be their own book about your trip. They can decorate the front and then draw special pictures of the things they like best about the trip. You might want to make a tradition of this. And then take the books out occasionally and reminisce over good memories of your past trips and vacations.

19. Travel ABC. Each person sees how far he can go in the alphabet in a specified amount of time—perhaps one-half hour. A person may claim a letter when he sees something that starts with that letter. For example he may see an animal. Animal starts with the letter A so he has the first letter and may move on to B. Each person follows this procedure calling out his letters until the time limit is up. The person who has gone farthest in the alphabet wins. This can also be done with words on billboards.

20. Colors. Let very young children look for colors. Any time they see a color they recognize, they say the name of that color aloud.

21. You won't believe this. In this activity everyone tells a "tall tale." Each person makes up the most ridiculous story he can imagine. Our family has lots of fun with this activity. You'll be amazed how quietly everyone listens to these family fantasies.

22. Continued story. Have someone start a story. At any point during the story that person may stop and the person on his right continues the story where he left off. The last member of the family must conclude the story. This can be lots of fun. Repeat it several times if your family enjoys the activity.

23. Memorize Scripture together. Travel time is a great time to memorize God's Word together. Select a Scripture verse such as Ephesians 4:32; Philippians 2:3-4; Colossians 3:2 and James 1:19. Repeat the verse aloud, phrase by phrase until you know it well. You might want to set a goal of memorizing the Scriptures I have just mentioned during your trip. These verses, if lived out, will certainly make your trip more enjoyable. Talk about each Scripture. Discuss: What does it mean? Why is it important to practice? How could it benefit the family?

24. Have family devotions. Take time each day you travel in the car to have family devotions. Read and discuss a portion of Scripture, or if your children are very young, read from a Bible storybook.

25. Take an interest in those you meet. Some good friends of ours, the John Drew family from Napa, California, took a bicentennial trip to some great historical points in the U.S. One of their goals as a family was to meet as many people as possible. The Drews taught their children how to meet strangers and engage them in interesting conversation by asking questions such as "Where do you live?", "What is the main industry in your state?", "What is the weather like?", and "What is your occupation?"

This was a great family adventure because the Drews were interested not only in significant places but in people. You can teach your children to become interested in others by giving them some guidelines before you leave on vacation. Of course, your example is very important. If you show an interest in people, they will too.

26. Surprise bag. All children, young and older, like surprises, so why not take along a surprise bag? Each day of the trip, if behavior has been appropriate (every parent has the privilege of some bribing) each child gets a surprise from the surprise bag. You could include such things as color books, snacks, and small toys. You can also have family items that you can save and take on future trips, such as special travel-size games like peg chess, peg checkers, or battleship.

27. Craziest thing I saw. Tell family members that they are to look for something very unusual during the next 50 miles. At the end of that time ask for reports. Vote as a family on who saw the "craziest thing."

28. Car count. Let each family member choose a make of car. During the next half hour see who can count the most cars of his make.

Now for Your Next Trip
I suggest that you read this chapter again before your next trip or vacation. You might even want to read it aloud as a family and decide on activities together. Plan some activities to do each day. Be sure to take this book along. During the trip give each child a chance to pick an activity from the book. Very soon your family will find things they will want to do

often. Most of all, I hope all of your trips and vacations are great adventures.

5

Celebrations of Special and Not-so-special Occasions

Every family has its special occasions—holidays, birthdays, anniversaries. But there are many more non-special days, and we have found ways to turn some of them into family occasions that we remember with pleasure.

Non-Occasion Celebrations
"What do you mean, 'Would I like to have a party next week'? What's the special occasion?" asked Liesl.

"No special occasion," replied Janet. "I just thought you might like to have a party for some of your friends."

"Wow! That would be great. Thanks, Mom. A party when there is no special occasion!"

Occasionally we like to do just that—let our girls have a party on a "not special occasion." We want our home to be a special place where our children will want to spend time and where they will want to bring friends.

This can happen in any family. All it takes is a desire on the part of parents, a little time, not a few frustrations, and an openness to new adventures. These adventures are worth the effort. They not only help make a happy family now but build memories that our children will look back on in adult life. These memories of good times past are what give children the strength and security to face struggles with their own families. The more positive memories we can add to our children's "album" of memories, the better. Equipped with these, they will be ready to face life. Here are some ideas with which you can build memories on those not-so-special occasions.

1. *"Just Because You're Home" Party.* Remember the story of the Prodigal Son? (Luke 15:11-32) He had squandered his inheritance, so he returned home to ask if he could be one of his father's servants. But no, his father would hear nothing of it. His son had returned, and that called for a great celebration.

The brother who had stayed home, worked hard and remained loyal, however, had a hard time with this. "Dad, you've never done this for me, and I have always been faithful."

My wife and I were discussing this story one day and she said, "You know, Wayne, I feel sorry for the other brother. Why didn't the father ever have a celebration for him, just because he was faithful? Why don't we have a 'just because you're home' party for our girls; a celebration to show how we appreciate them?"

She's right. Why do we wait so long to show our appreciation to our children in special ways? After they leave home, then we are motivated. We wish they would return for special times—but then it's too late. They have their own interests. So why not now?

A "just because you're home" celebration can be very simple. A nice dinner, a special dessert that your children will enjoy. Read Luke 15:11-32 at the dinner table. There are several ways you can show your appreciation. Think of several special qualities that each of your children has and share them. You might even want to select a Scripture verse that you feel represents each one. Finish the following sentence for each of your children. *(Child's name),* just because you're home, our family *(insert some contribution your child makes to the family).*

Perhaps you could set aside extra money and enjoy some recreation together that night. Like bowling, skating, a good movie, or swimming. A small gift of some kind could really set the evening apart as something your children will always remember.

This is not just for little children. It doesn't hurt a bit to show appreciation to your teenagers. Just adapt these ideas to their age-level or think up some you know your teenagers will enjoy.

2. *Plant a candy tree.* This activity works well with younger children—preschool through elementary. I've done this several times with our children. I buy a bag of wrapped candy. Sometime during our day out, usually in the woods or at a park, I sneak off and find a small tree or bush on which I can place the candy. I attach the candy carefully to the limbs, within reach of the children, and then call loudly "I've found a candy tree." The children come running because they know what this means. They strip the tree of all its candy and go happily back to their activities.

When Bridget was small she could never really figure this out. She would say, "Daddy, is that really a candy tree, or did you put the candy on it?"

I gave her one of my sly grins that says, "I've got a secret" and kidded, "What do you think, Bridget? Wouldn't it be fun to believe in candy trees?"

3. *Destination unknown.* You can do this anytime. Select a destination that you know your children will enjoy. In the summertime you could pack a special picnic lunch. Just tell your children that you are going someplace very special. The suspense will "kill" them. When you arrive at your secret destination, eat your picnic lunch and play some good old-fashioned games like freeze tag, kick-the-can, hide-and-seek, softball, or touch football.

4. *Pig trough.* Invite several families into your home or maybe try this at a party you give for your children. Purchase from a building supply store a 10′ section of gutter. Line the

gutter with aluminum foil. Fill a section of gutter (how much depends on the size of your group) with different flavors of ice cream and topping, then let the "pigs" go at it. Use spoons, of course. This will be a memory that your children, and you, will never forget.

5. *Early morning jog.* Surprise your family early some morning by waking them up and announcing, "The family is going to jog together." Don't try to jog beyond your family's endurance. In fact, just a rapid walk might do it for some families. After the jog, fix a hearty breakfast for the family. Some families might want to go out for breakfast.

6. *Family holidays.* Last summer while on our vacation, we were eating lunch in a park. A rather stiff wind blew Bridget's napkin away. She ran after it, but it continued to elude her. We laughed and laughed as Bridget wore herself out trying to catch the napkin. She finally succeeded, and we gave her a big cheer as she finally panted back with a tattered napkin in her hand. "This is such a great occasion," I joked, "that we must make a family holiday out of it. Let's call it 'Bridget Caught the Napkin Day.' "

Believe it or not, this crazy holiday has caught on. We now celebrate "Bridget Caught the Napkin Day." Use your creativity. Why not celebrate a special day each year for each of your children? It could be something silly, or something meaningful, like one of your children's accomplishments. Perhaps "Tom's All-'A' Day" or "Ruth's Pleasant Smile Day" (celebrating the fact that Ruth usually has a pleasant smile). The celebrations for these family holidays do not have to be elaborate but your children will really enjoy the attention of having a holiday named after them.

7. *Swimming party.* In our town we can rent the high school pool for no more than three large pizzas would cost. One evening we decided to rent it and invited several families in the church to enjoy it with us. Afterwards we had refreshments at our house. We simply had a great time with a pool all to ourselves. We plan on making this an annual affair.

Inquire about the pools in your area and see if they have similar accommodations.

8. *Whatever day.* What about an unplanned day? Call it "Whatever Day." Just get in the car and launch out on an adventure with no plans whatsoever. Decide what direction you want to go. Stop when you see something that looks interesting. Take your time. Relax and take time for the things you are usually too busy for, such as parks, secondhand stores or "whatever."

9. *Shrinky Dink time.* To turn a not-so-special time into something exciting for your children, try making Shrinky Dinks. Shrinky Dink is the brand name for a plastic craft material that shrinks when heated. You can buy kits at the store and have a delightful time making name tags, key chains, necklaces, pins, and so on.

You trace whatever you feel is appropriate on the transparent material with a permanent marking pen or colored pencil, and then heat. If you have an oven with a window you can watch a real show as these pieces of plastic curl up and shrink.

You can achieve the same shrinking effect by using plastic lids. Just trace on the lid with a permanent felt-tip pen and heat.

10. *Favorite-family night.* Some of my fondest memories of childhood were when we invited families to our house. I notice that our children value these times with other families also. This is one of the great benefits of being part of the family of God—having times together with others who serve Christ.

Why not schedule a once-a-month favorite-family night? Perhaps let each child, in turn, choose his favorite family to invite. You do not need to make elaborate preparations for this time of fellowship. Just some dessert, popcorn, a game if appropriate, and some good talk.

Assign the child who invited the family the task of being host or hostess for the night. He should welcome the guests at the door, take their coats, perhaps serve dessert and any other duties you might think of that are associated with favorite family night.

11. Game Night. If you are a family that does not play games much, you might want occasionally to have a game night. Why not add some excitement to this night and decide as a family on a new game to buy and play? If this doesn't appeal to you, decide on one of your old favorites to play.

12. Family memory night. Set aside a night, at least once a year, to reflect on good family memories of great times past. If you have slides or pictures, show them. Have fun thinking back on the good times your family has had together. Have each family member tell what he thinks is the best time the family has ever had together.

Special Activities for Families with Young Children

1. Zoo night. Each family member decides on an animal he would like to be. He must act like that animal. The rest of the family tries to guess what animal that person is. Read an interesting animal story to your children. The story of Bambi is always popular.

Next, have an animal hunt. Hide animal crackers in one room. You might want to wrap them in paper. Tell the children that wild animals are all over the room and they are to "hunt" them down. Have fun eating the animals that have been found.

2. Bake cookies night. If you can stand the mess, this is a great activity for younger children. Dad, don't try to duck out of this activity. Your presence is essential. Let your children help roll out the dough and cut the cookies. The best time of all, however, will be eating those delicious creations. End the evening by taking some of the cookies to a neighbor, or better yet, to an older couple or shut-in in your church.

3. Dress-up night. I'm sure by now you know how young children like to play dress-up. Get some old suits and ties for your boys. For your girls supply old dresses, high heels, jewelry, etc. Then have a great time letting them dress up and parade before you. You might even want to have a style show.

Now let me share something that we did at our house that was completely hilarious. Bridget wanted me to dress up. That's right—and in women's clothes, no less! Can you imagine what I looked like when Bridget finally paraded her prized creation before the rest of the family? It will never happen to me again, but I dare you to try it just once, Dads!

4. Circus night. We tried this and it worked very well. Each family member was required to do a circus act. I remember that mine was the most daring of all. I walked a tight rope. Although the rope was laid on the floor, my winning performance had the entire family in suspense. Will he make it? We ended the evening by eating delicious circus novelty desserts.

5. Fishing well night. This is an all-time favorite for children both young and old. Simply hang a sheet or blanket across the door to one of your rooms about head height. To make a fishing rod, tie a string on a yardstick and tie a clothes pin on the end of the string. Now either Mom or Dad should stand behind the sheet to hook up the "fish." Each child should get several turns at fishing. Have some small surprises for them to fish out. Maybe a small Bible picture/storybook, candy, small toy animals, or whatever you might have handy. Beware! This type of evening can be habit-forming. Your children will want to "fish" over and over.

6. Foamy is fun. Your children won't believe it when you squirt out great gobs of foam (shaving cream) and tell them that they can play in it. I will never forget the first time Bridget was allowed to do this. She couldn't believe I was actually allowing her to play in something so delightfully messy. Save this one for the game room or garage.

There are various ways young children can have fun with foamy. You can put some on a piece of construction paper and let them use it as if it were finger paint. Or you can give them spoons, cups and other such items and just let them play. This is really what they like best. Of course, shaving cream is mostly soap so it cleans up easily. Warn your children not to rub it in their eyes.

Special Occasion Celebrations

1. Birthdays. Birthdays are very special times to children. The effort we put into making birthdays special are a visible sign of our love to our children.

Leisl returned from one of her friend's birthday parties one day and exclaimed, "That birthday party was nothing. No pretty napkins, no decorations, *and only a store-bought cake.*"

Janet has always made a real effort to make birthdays special at our house. Of course, every year she says, "Never again, it's too much of a hassle." But when the next birthday rolls around we have another very special day. The children really appreciate her efforts. They feel extra special on those days.

2. "Spiritual Birthdays." We feel that the day our children were born into God's family is more important than the day of their physical birth. We always decorate the house, have a birthday cake, and many times have friends in to help us celebrate. I always present some type of spiritual thought to encourage that person's spiritual growth during the following year.

We also buy a special spiritual birthday present. For Heidi one year it was an Avon key ring. For the spiritual thought I gave each person a paper key and had him write on that key a thought or Scripture verse that would be a "key" for the birthday person's spiritual growth. Each person then shared his thought and handed the key to Heidi.

This year for Liesl's spiritual birthday we gave her a picture of a horse, drawn by Joni. Joni is a Christian artist who was paralyzed in an accident. She draws by holding a pencil in her teeth. Since three members of the family had read the book *Joni*, they were asked to share some things they felt were significant in her life. Then we each tried to draw a picture holding a pencil in our teeth. We concluded the evening with each person praying that he would develop the strength of character that Joni demonstrated.

For our little one, Bridget, who has not yet made a decision for Jesus, we have a "Bridget Loves Jesus" night. This is celebrated like a spiritual birthday, but there is no specific time of the year that we celebrate.

3. Kids' Day. Have you ever heard your children say, "There is Mother's Day and a Father's Day, why isn't there a Kid's Day? There is. September 23 has been suggested as Kid's Day by Kiwanis International and the second Sunday of June is sometimes recognized as Children's Day. How about surprising your children by celebrating it this year? Do it up right—breakfast in bed (if you dare), the meal and dessert of their choice, and maybe even a family activity that they choose. Of course I should warn you, once you start celebrating "Kid's Day" you will probably have to celebrate it forever.

4. Father's Day and Mother's Day. These should be celebrated in a big way, giving the children a chance to show their love for Mom and Dad by doing special things. The parent who is not being honored should help the children organize this important time. It is almost a tradition in our home that when mother is honored the girls make a crown for her, give her a scepter, put a cape over her shoulders and seat her in a special chair. This year Heidi shared some Scriptures that showed how important God thinks mothers are. Then we served Mom her favorite dessert.

Here are a couple of activities you can use for both Mother's Day and Father's Day. Have a quiz about the person being honored. Give each family member a sheet of paper and have him list in a column the following: favorite song, time of day, dessert, food, part of house, sport, animal, movie, Scripture verse.

Opposite each item everyone should write what they think is the honored person's favorite song, time of day, etc. When everyone is finished, take an item at a time and have each person say what he thinks Mom or Dad's favorite thing was in that category. Mom or Dad then gives the correct answer. For each correct answer a person gets two points. See who knows Mom or Dad best.

Another activity is for each person to finish the following sentences. The thing I appreciate about (Mom or Dad) most is _____. (Mom or Dad) helps make this a happy home by _____. I will show my appreciation to (Mom or Dad) by doing the following during the next week _____.

5. *Graduations and anniversaries.* These are other special occasions for which you should plan purposeful activities. I suggest husbands and wives sit down together to plan. As you think together you will be amazed at the creative ideas you can come up with that will make these times lasting memories.

Everyone likes to be honored. Make special occasions out of things your children accomplish. Things like good report cards, participation in school and church events that take significant effort, helping others in specific ways, could all merit special recognition.

You can honor a child in various ways—a special dinner serving his favorite food, or a small gift. Another thing that works well is to make a banner or pennant with your child's name on it. You could make one for each child and "fly" it when that child has done something special (maybe even when a child has a good week at helping around the house).

You can turn special and not-so-special occasions into warm family memories in many ways. I'm sure you have family celebrations that give you great joy. Think over the ideas in the chapter—choose a few that you can add to your growing family album of memories for your children.

6

Family Activities
That Say "I Care"

How long has it been since you heard one of your children say
to his brother or sister, "I love you"?

"What?" you say. "Brothers and sisters just don't do that."
I'll agree that it seldom happens in most families. It's not that
brothers and sisters don't love or appreciate one another, for I
really believe in most cases they do. It's just that children do
not naturally think about expressing their love and appreciation to each other. Wouldn't it be great if our children would
express positive sentiments about each other as creatively as
they do the things that bug them!

I believe we can teach family members to appreciate one
another and to express it verbally. The most obvious way is
through your example. How often do your children hear you
express your love and appreciation for your spouse? Do you
say as many positive things about your children as you do
negative ones? Do you praise your children daily? By expressing love to children in word as well as action, we teach them
to express their love in the same way.

Another way we can teach them to express their appreciation to one another is through carefully structured family
times that say "I care." Let's take a look at some ideas for
family times in which we show our love for each other.

Family Times That Express Love

Our good friends, the John Drew family, have a family time each week that says "I care." Each Wednesday evening, their regular family night, in addition to family night activities, a family member is honored.

John, the father, begins by telling the meaning of the honoree's name. He then praises certain qualities in that person's life and sometimes shares a Scripture that represents that family member. Then each family member, in turn, says something he appreciates about the person being honored. The children are encouraged to look past outward characteristics such as pretty eyes, nice hair, etc. and focus on inner qualities such as kindness, diligence, etc.

"I believe this is the most important thing we have ever done in our family," John recently told me. "The children never tire of their 'special night.' I believe that this has been a great boost to their self-esteem."

"And by the way, Wayne," John continued, "each family member is honored including Carol (John's wife), and I feel it is just as important for parents to be honored as it is for children."

Family times that say "I care" help family members to verbalize their appreciation to one another, and this builds self-esteem. A good combination! I'd like to share with you some ideas for family times that say "I care."

1. Build a house. Write each family member's name on a slip of paper. Put the slips in a container and have each person draw one. Next give everyone a sheet of typing paper, pencils, and magic markers. Explain that family members are to draw a house for the one whose name they drew, as they feel that one would like it. It should be furnished and decorated in a way that reflects the tastes of the person for whom it is being drawn.

When we did this in our family, my oldest daughter, Heidi, got my name. She did a really good job of drawing a house that I would like—large family room, elaborately-decorated den with a large desk. But the moment of truth came when I saw my kitchen. There was an oversized refrigerator with guess-who standing there ready to open it. I could have done without that reminder of one of my vices.

When each person has completed his house he should show it to the rest of the family, explaining why he drew the rooms a certain way, chose colors, decorated, etc. The person for whom the house was built should then comment on how well the house depicts his personality. Discuss how each person in the family is different. Take a few moments to thank God for making each family member unique.

2. *Advertising each other.* Write your family members' names on slips of paper. Put them in a container and have each person draw a name. Give each person a 2 x 2 foot section of butcher paper or a piece of poster board. Tell family members that they are to make an advertisement about the person whose name they drew. Have a lot of different kinds of magazines available, marking pens, scissors, and glue.

Family members may make their advertisements in any way they wish—pictures of things the person likes to do, his qualities, etc. When the advertisements have been completed, each person should try to "sell" his product. For example, if I had drawn Bridget's name, I would have pasted pictures all about her—things she liked, her favorite foods, hobbies, qualities—on the poster paper. Then I would explain the poster, trying to "sell" the rest of the family on what a great person Bridget is.

3. *Honor scrapbook.* One evening a mother showed me a good idea for a family time that says "I care." It was an "Honor Dad scrapbook." The mother explained, "Our children made this for their Dad on "honor your father" family night. The children cut out magazine pictures that reminded them of Dad. They pasted the pictures in the scrapbook. Under each picture there was a statement such as "Dad likes camping."

As I looked at this scrapbook of love, one picture caught

my eye. It was a picture of a man and woman embracing. Under that picture were the words "Daddy loves Mommy."

This would be an excellent project to honor your children. Work on this together with your spouse. You could cut out pictures, use old photographs, momentos, or write little stories of interesting things your children have done. Then, on a special honor night, go through the honor scrapbook with your child. This could be repeated over the years.

4. A poem about you. You don't have to be a real poet to write a poem about another family member. Just have family members exchange names and make a simple four-line poem such as:

> Liesl can shoot a basketball
> Or run a very fast race.
> I'll admit she's very small
> But she sets a very fast pace.

5. An acrostic about you. Have each person write the person's name you want to honor in acrostic form on a piece of paper as shown in the sketch. Have each family member think of a quality of the honoree that begins with each letter in his name. Then share the acrostics with the one being honored.

> L—Lively
> I—Interesting
> E—Enthusiastic
> S—Sweet
> L—Likeable

6. Appreciation night. Give each person a sheet of paper with a wheel on it, as shown in Figure 4. Each person is to enter his own name in the inner circle. He then passes his circle to the person on his left who writes in one section what he appreciates about that person and signs his name. He then passes it on the next person who also writes what he appreciates about the one whose name is on the inner circle. This process continues until each person has written what he appreciates about each family member. The circles are returned

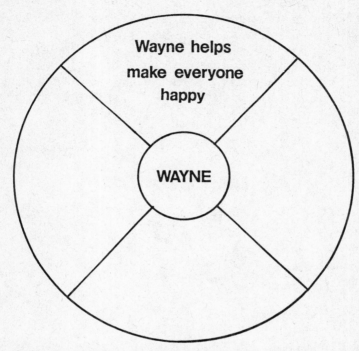

to their owners. Each person, in turn, then reads aloud what the other members of the family appreciate about him.

Family members might want to keep these as a reminder that they really are loved and appreciated by other family members.

7. *A letter of appreciation.* We write letters of appreciation to others; why not to those who are closest to us—our family members. Take an evening to write letters of appreciation to one another. Of course, younger children will write very short letters, while older children should be able to write longer ones. The length is not as important as the fact that they put their thoughts on paper. If a child is having problems thinking of things he appreciates about another family member, you might want to help him by asking questions such as,

"What makes the person special?" "Does he ever do anything for you?" "What does he do that makes other people happy?"

8. *Flower honor activity*. Choose a family member to be honored, and have your family make a flower for that one. Draw a flower on construction paper and cut out the center and petals as shown in Figure 5. Write the person's name on

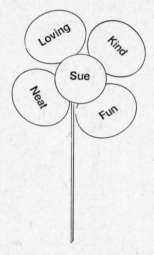

the center piece and give it to him. Give a petal to the other family members. Each family member is to write on the petal what he appreciates about the honoree and give it to him. The one being honored then pastes the petals on the center piece and keeps it as a reminder of his family's love for him.

9. *Play compliments*. This is a game that gives family members an opportunity to show appreciation for one another while having fun. Send one person from the room. The rest of the family writes compliments about the absent person. The person who left the room is called back and one person reads all the compliments to that person, who is to try and guess who wrote each one. Each family member should have a turn being complimented.

10. *Dress me up.* Here is an activity that even the little ones will enjoy. Cut a life-sized piece of butcher paper or newspaper roll end for each member of your family. Have each person lie down (on his back) on the paper. Trace an outline of the person on the paper. When each family member has been traced, write your family member's names on slips of paper. Draw names. Each person is to take the outline of the person whose name he drew, and color in all the details. He should draw clothes he feels that person would like. Each person can add jewelry, facial features, hair color, and any other details. Crayons or magic markers work well for this project. Your children will be sure to "overdress" the person whose name they drew. You will have a great time laughing over these pictures.

11. *Stick-figure appreciation.* Do this activity around your table. Give each family member a piece of typing paper. Have everyone fold the paper in fourths. Draw names. Then have family members draw a stick-figure story of the person whose name they drew. Each person should have four scenes to his story, one for each square on the paper. Share these stories with one another.

12. *Share a burden—bear a burden.* Read Galatians 6:2. Discuss: What is a burden? What does it mean to "bear one another's burdens"? Starting with yourself, share a burden with the person on your left. That person should say, "I will help you bear that burden." Then, depending on the burden, he should say what he is going to do, perhaps pray for you each day or help in some other way. Next the "burden bearer" shares his burden with the person on his left. Repeat until each person shares and bears a burden.

13. *A people paper project.* Give each family member a regular-size piece of typing paper. Write each person's name on a slip of paper and draw names. Everyone is to fold, tear, or manipulate his piece of paper in such a way that it will tell something about the person whose name he drew. For example, if I drew Liesl (our 11-year-old daughter) I might roll

the paper in a ball to represent the fact that she loves to play basketball.

When each person has completed the project, go around the family circle with each person explaining how the person whose name he drew is like his piece of paper.

14. Family drama. Choose one person and explain that the rest of the family is going to do a drama about him. While that person waits, take the rest of the family into another room and plan your drama. Decide what event in that person's life you want to dramatize. It could be a great accomplishment or you might want to choose an embarrassing moment. When you have planned the mini-drama, perform it for the waiting family member. You might want to do a drama on each family member.

15. Great moments in your life. Every family member has had his "great and memorable moments." Mom or Dad can share some of these moments at the dinner table occasionally. This type of activity can help build positive self-esteem and family unity.

16. The king—the queen. This activity is for children seven and under. Allow your child to be "king" or "queen" for the evening. Let him sit in the middle of the room while the family sings for him the following lines to the tune of "Row, Row, Row, Your Boat." Fill in the blanks with the appropriate information.

> Heidi, Heidi Rickerson
> (insert your child's name)
> You are very special.
> Your eyes are _____
> Your hair is _____
> We love you just like that!

17. Things I appreciate. Have your family draw names. During the next week each person is to look for good qualities in the person whose name he drew. Keep a list. At the end of the week have family members share their lists. Who found the most positive qualities?

18. You're like this object. Each family member is to find an object that reminds him in some way of a quality in each other member of the family. For example, I might find a flower for my wife. I would choose this object for her because it would symbolize her efforts to make the house beautiful. For Bridget, I would find a picture of a person because of her love for people.

Communicating feelings of love and appreciation to family members is an ongoing process. Structured family time activities will help. Spontaneous sharing of love and appreciation is also important. Your example as a parent is vital. You can create a climate in your home in which the sharing of love and appreciation among family members happens regularly.

7
Three Games to Make and Play

Are you willing to spend a couple of hours preparing some exciting games for your family? If your answer is Yes this chapter is for you. Your family will get many hours of enjoyment playing these three games.

We developed them as a family project. Our goal was to create easy-to-make, purposeful, and entertaining—if not hilarious—games to play.

We have helped hundreds of other families make these games. The feedback is always the same, "Our children love playing these games," or "Our family has been drawn closer together because of these games." So we hope you will take the time to make and play them. The games are designed to build memories, develop family relationships, and teach Christian values—goals I feel all families should work toward in every way possible.

Look the games over and decide which one you will make first. Some families might want to make the games as a family project (perhaps on family night). For other families it might be best for the husband and wife to make the game.

The Family Memory-maker Game

Memories of good times together as a family are important.

Character and self-image are built, in part, from childhood memories. This game is designed to help you build memories in your family.

The Family Memory-Maker Game is a different kind of game. In most games you compete. In this game you *co-operate*. It focuses on helping one another rather than competing within the family. The only competition is against the clock. This game should help you communicate, know and understand one another better, show love, and have fun as a family.

How to Make the Game

Take a piece of graph paper and lay a regular size (8½" x 11") piece of typing paper over it. Make your game board by drawing in equal-size blocks as shown in Figure 6. Write the instruction on the appropriate blocks.

You may find it easier to play the game if it is larger than a piece of typing paper. Either draw an enlarged version, or locate a process camera—at a print shop or at your school resource center—and make a copy of Figure 6 to the size you want. You can then mount it on posterboard and add your own colorful lettering and drawings.

Next write the following statements on 3" x 5" index cards. Lay these cards face down next to your game board. You will also need one marker and one die.

Statements for Your 3" x 5" Cards
- Act out a characteristic of one family member. If guessed, move ahead one space (30 seconds to guess).
- The Bible says, "bear one another's burdens" (Gal. 6:2). Tell about your biggest problem. Each family member, in turn, must give you one idea to help you solve the problem.
- Your family has just inherited $5,000 from a rich uncle. Decide how it will be spent.

The (Rickersons')

FAMILY MEMORY - MAKER GAME

Welcome Home

Unless the Lord builds the house,
they labor in vain who build it
Psalm 127:1 (nasb).

Start

14 You're happy! Go ahead five.
13
12 Sad face. Tickle one another.
11
10 Family hassle. Go back two.
9 Avoid a quarrel. Go ahead one.
8
7
6 Chirp like a bird.
5
4 God loves you. Go ahead one.
3
2 Got angry. Go back one.
1

15
16 Forgave your brother. Go ahead one.
17
18 Messy bedrooms. Go ahead one.
19 Love is kind. Go ahead one.
20 Tired of sitting? Crawl to bedroom and back.
21
22
23
24 Acted impatiently. Go back one.

25
26 Everyone whistle favorite song.
27
28 Ate too much. Go back one.
29
30 Obeyed Mother. Go ahead one.
31
32 Returned evil for evil. Go back three.
33
34 Everyone changes places.
35
36 Pray for one another. Go ahead one.
37
38 Tattled on sis. Go back one.
39
40 Everyone run around the house.
41
42 Spoke a soft word. Go ahead one.
43
44 Everyone howl like a wolf.
45
46 Listened carefully. Go ahead one.
47
48 Yawn.
49 Scream if you feel like it.
50
51
52

- Agree on three words that best describe the ideal father.
- If you could change one thing about yourself, what would it be? Each family member must agree or disagree that it needs to be changed.
- What is your best family memory (experience)? If the entire family agrees in one minute, you may move ahead two spaces.
- Agree on three words that best describe the ideal mother.
- Agree on three words that best describe the ideal child.
- If the world was to end in one hour, what would be your final activity?
- Think of someone with whom the entire family is well acquainted and describe how you feel about him. If the family can identify the person in one minute, you may move ahead three spaces.
- What is your greatest wish? If each family member gives you a good suggestion on how to get that wish, move ahead three spaces.
- Find a feather. Together as a family, blow upward on the feather, and see how long you can keep it up in the air.
- Join hands in a circle of prayer with each person praying for the person on his left.
- Pantomime a Bible character. If guessed in one minute, move ahead one space.
- Pantomime a Bible animal. If guessed in 30 seconds, move ahead one space.
- Each person should go to his room and get a pillow. For the next two minutes have a family pillow fight.
- The Bible says to "honor thy father." Father must leave the room, and the family must decide in two minutes how they will honor father tonight.
- If you could have any person, either dead or alive, as a guest in your home, who would it be? If you can agree in 30 seconds, move ahead one space.
- Guess a family member's favorite color.

- Have each person say which is his favorite room in the house. Then see if there is a favorite family room.
- Say "I love you" to each family member in a different way (hug, kiss, smile, etc.)
- The Bible says to encourage our leaders (1 Thes. 5:12-13). Decide together on a church leader you would like to encourage. Telephone him now and say a word of appreciation.
- Have each family member complete this sentence: "I get a sad feeling when . . ."
- Have each family member complete this sentence: "I am most likely to get angry when . . ."
- Have each family member complete the following sentence: "I am usually afraid when . . ."
- Have each family member complete the following sentence: "I am most happy when . . ."
- Ephesians 4:32 says that we should be kind to one another. Each family member should say one way that he will be kind to a family member during the next week.
- All family members must laugh constantly during the next 60 seconds. If they do this, you may move ahead one space.
- Choose a family member and have the rest of the family guess what his/her favorite hymn is.
- Fire drill!!! Each person should go to his room and bring back the thing he would take with him in case of fire. Tell why. If done in three minutes, you may move ahead three spaces.
- The Bible says to "Be thankful in all circumstances." Agree on a family disappointment to thank God for.
- Decide together what large animal Dad should be. Each child can have a ride.
- Romans 12:13 says that we are to open our homes to strangers. Decide now on a family in the church or neighborhood whose members are strangers to you, and invite them to your house for dinner or dessert.

- God's Word says not to quarrel (Prov. 17:14). When was your last family quarrel, and how can it be avoided in the future?
- Exchange a piece of clothing with the person on your left and wear it for the rest of the game.
- Each family member must find a hat and wear it for the rest of the game.
- Raid the cookie jar—each person may have two cookies.
- You are the leader. Family members must do as you do for the next three minutes.
- Each person must find a book, bring it back, and create a new title for it. If this can be done in three minutes, move ahead three spaces.
- If Jesus had written a book, what might have been its title and the titles of the first and last chapters? Each person should reply.
- Each family member should think of a nickname for the family member on his right. If this activity is completed in 30 seconds, you may move ahead one space.

How to Play the Game

The object of the game is to move from Start to Welcome Home while trying to understand and cooperate with one another as much as possible. Only one marker is used; it is for the whole family. Each person will take a turn moving the marker.

1. To start the game, one family member draws a card, reads it aloud, and the family cooperates to follow the instructions.

2. When the activity on the card is completed, the card is placed on a discard pile, and the die is rolled (the same person who drew the card rolls the die).

3. This same person moves the marker the number of spaces shown on the die. Follow any instructions that are written on the block on which you land. After this two-step process, the next player gets a turn. *Remember questions and*

activities are for the entire family to do together—not just the person whose turn it is.

4. Each player, in turn, follows instructions 1-3. Continue the game with each family member taking a turn until you have reached Home. We suggest that you end the game with a circle of prayer. (The Memory-Maker Game, Wayne Rickerson © 1976)

Talk Blocks

You will have family fun and excitement as you make and play this simple game. You need only a 2 x 2 x 2 inch cube of wood and some easy-to-find letters and pictures. Building supply stores have 2 x 2 boards which you can purchase for a reasonable amount. Simply mark off 2" blocks and cut as many as you will need.

Your talk block, when finished, will have a picture or writing on each of its six sides. Four sides are Bible categories and two sides are designed to promote discussion and family sharing.

Here's what to put on the six sides of your block. On side one glue a picture of a Bible woman—just the head will do. Your children's Sunday School papers are a great place to find these pictures. You can also find appropriate pictures in sticker books at your Christian bookstore.

On side two glue a picture of a Bible man. On side three, a picture of a Bible town (this could be a small section of a Bible lands map). On side four place a Bible animal; on side five glue a large "S," and on side six a large "L." (Elmer's Glue works well.)

How to Play

Now that you have built your "talk block," here's how to play. Have your family sit in a close circle on the floor. One person rolls the block as he would a die. If a Bible category turns up, *the first person* to say something in that category is the next to roll. For example, if a family member were to roll

"Bible man," the first person to shout out the name of a Bible man gets to roll the block next. Once something or someone has been named it cannot be repeated during the game.

The same procedure is followed when someone rolls the other three Bible categories—Bible woman, Bible town, Bible animal.

The S side of your block is noncompetitive and can be used in two ways. (1) The person who rolls S is to share something—a blessing, a problem, a thought, etc.—with the rest of the family, or (2) the person who rolls S may receive a special surprise (you might want to do both). What I usually do is have some change on the floor beside me. I put a penny, a nickel, or a dime in the center and when someone rolls an S he gets that amount. Snacks can also be used for the surprise. Your children will love the surprise side.

The L side of your block is also noncompetitive. The L stands for like. The person who rolls the L says one thing he likes about the person on his left. Then each family member, in turn, tells one thing he likes about the person on his left. The person who rolled the L gets to roll again.

We usually set a 15-minute time limit for our game. When the time is up (we set the buzzer on the stove), the person who is in possession of the block rolls it one more time and shares a thought based on whatever turns up. We then conclude with each person in the family praying a sentence prayer.

Categories for the Blocks
Make several "Talk Blocks." The potential is unlimited. There are many categories you can put on the blocks. I suggest that you always have at least two noncompetitive sides. Here are some categories that I have used: combine them in any way you wish on your blocks. Find pictures or letters to represent the categories you choose, and glue them on a block.

1. *Competitive:*
   • Water—Name a body of water mentioned in the Bible.
   • Bible Object—Name an object mentioned in the Bible.

- Plague—Name one of the 10 plagues.
- Bible Mountain—Name a Bible mountain.
- Bible Parable—Name one of Jesus' parables.
- Bible Proverb—Quote one of the proverbs.
- Bible Promise—Name a promise given in the Bible.
- Bible Commandment—Quote one of the Ten Commandments.
- Bible Pair—Name two persons who are mentioned together in the Bible.
- A few more possibilities are—Bible plant, Bible insect, Bible occupation, Bible book (name a book in the Bible), Bible king, Bible miracle.

2. *Noncompetitive:*

- Draw a question mark—the person who rolls this may ask a question of anyone else in the family.
- Draw a heart—the person who rolls this must say "I love you" to the person on his left. Each family member in turn says "I love you" to the person on his left.
- Draw some music notes—the person who rolls this starts his favorite song and the family sings it together.
- Draw a large *P*. The person who rolls *P* must praise God for something.
- Draw a smiley face—the person who rolls this must finish the sentence "Happiness is _____."

(Talk Blocks, Wayne Rickerson, © 1976)

Spin the Bottle

Parents of preschoolers take note. This is a game the little ones will enjoy as much as the older children do. This game is very easy to make and play. All you need is a stack of 3" x 5" index cards and a soft drink bottle.

Here's how the game is played. The family sits in a circle on the floor. One person starts the game by spinning the bottle. The person to whom the bottle points draws a card, reads it, follows the directions, and places the card at the bottom of the stack. (Of course, with preschool children, an older person will have to read the card.) If the card drawn is a fact question, then the person who drew it must answer correctly to qualify to spin the bottle. If he can't think of the answer within a set time, the person on his left may answer, and so on until someone answers correctly. The person who answers correctly gets to spin the bottle.

If the card does not require an answer, then the person to whom the bottle pointed does what is required on the card and spins the bottle.

Select from these suggestions those that fit the ages of your children, and make up others of your own.

- Tickle one another.
- Play hide-and-seek for five minutes.
- The entire family must go outside and run around the house.
- Name the first man and woman on earth.
- Can you name Jesus' mother and father?
- Who was the shepherd boy who became king? If you're correct, spin again.
- Name two of Jesus' disciples. Spin again if you know.
- Who was the boy who helped Eli in the temple? If correct, spin again.
- Can you name a Bible food? Spin again if you can.
- What was the name of the giant David killed? If you know, spin again.
- Think of a Bible person and give a clue. The rest of the family must guess whom you're thinking of.
- Do a puppet show.
- The Bible says, "Obey your parents." Mother can tell you one thing to do now and you must obey her.
- Draw a picture and send it to your Grandpa and Grandma. (You may wish to postpone this activity until the game is completed.)
- BONANZA! Dad must take everyone out for a treat *now*! (End of game, everyone wins.)
- Go to your room (all children). When Mom and Dad

call, you can come back in and find special surprises they have hidden.

- Where was Jesus born? Spin again if you know.
- What was Moses' sister's name? If you know you can spin again.
- What kind of work did Jesus' father do? Spin again if you know.
- Who had a coat of many colors? If you know, spin again.
- God made everything. Tell one thing God has made that you like.
- Think of an animal that Noah took on the ark. Make a noise like that animal. The person who guesses what kind of animal you are may spin next.
- God wants us to be happy. Laugh as loud as you can.
- You may ask a Bible question. The person who answers correctly may spin the bottle.
- Turn a somersault.
- Stand on your head.
- The Bible is God's special Book. Tell your favorite Bible story.
- Go to the kitchen and get a cookie for each family member.
- God wants children to love their mothers. Give your mother a kiss and a hug and say, "I love you."
- God wants children to love their fathers. Give your father a kiss and a hug and say, "I love you."
- Who is your favorite Bible man?
- Who is your favorite Bible woman?
- Love is kind. Do something kind for the person closest to you.
- Jesus said, "Follow Me." Play follow-the-leader. You are the leader. Family members must follow you for the next three minutes.
- Make a joyful noise unto the Lord. Have a family rhythm band. Each family member should get a "musical instrument" (pot, pan, stick, spoon, bottle).

- Pantomime a Bible story.
- The whole family wrestles on the floor for the next three minutes. (Or pair up to arm-wrestle.)
- Go to your room and bring back the toy you like best. Show it to the family. Tell why you like it.
- Tell Dad to do something funny.
- Tell Mom to do something funny.
- Jesus loves you. Sing "Jesus Loves Me" for the family.
- The Bible says friends are important. Who is your best friend?
- Jesus says we are to help others. Have you helped someone today? If so, you can spin again.
- There is a special surprise for you. Ask your father where it is and share it with the rest of the family. (Be sure there *is* a surprise prepared.)
- What is your favorite color? Find something in the room that is your favorite color.
- Dad is to be your horse. Each child can ride him two times around the room.
- Make a funny face.
- Each family member must find a hat to wear for the rest of the game.
- Tickle Mom or Dad.
- God made pets. Go get your pet and do a trick with him for the family.
- Mother must bark like a dog.

8

Simple Games for Family Fun

Some of our best times as a family have been when we have played simple games together. In this chapter I'm going to share some of our favorites with you. Often we will play one of these games on a family night. Other times we will play a game after dinner or perhaps on a Friday evening.

It's good to have a list of games that the family enjoys. If you have such a list, you will probably find games in this chapter that you will want to add to it. If you do not have one, I suggest that you use this chapter to help you begin.

These games take little or no preparation, involve plenty of action and are just plain fun. Read through this chapter and put a check mark by the games you feel your family will enjoy. The next time you are tempted to reach for the TV knob, try one of these games instead, and see if old-fashioned family fun isn't still the best family time of all.

1. Table hockey. Even hear of table hockey? I hadn't either, until a few months ago when a friend, Skip Centioli, explained the fun he had playing the game with his wife, two teenage sons and five-year-old daughter.

It sounded like a good idea to me so we tried it on our next family night. The girls loved it. Here's how it's played: place two pieces of tape four inches apart on each end of your kitchen or dining room table as shown in Figure 7. A Ping-Pong ball makes a good puck. Divide your family into two

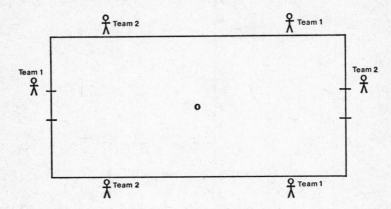

teams. You will need a minimum of four persons. If your family has an odd number, one of the younger children could help a teammate or Mom or Dad serve as scorekeeper and referee.

Assign goals and put opposing team members at each end of the table to defend their goal. Position the other players on either side of the table. Each team tries to blow the Ping-Pong ball through the opening between the tape strips on the opposing team's goal. When successful, the team scores *three* points for the goal. If the Ping-Pong ball does not go through the goal but goes off the *end* of the table, the team trying to score the goal receives *one* point. If the ball goes off the side of the table, no points are scored, the ball is placed in the center of the table, and both sides blow on the ball again. Play this game for 15 minutes or until one family member faints from lack of air.

2. Box bowling. This game has been so popular with our children that they have asked me to lead it at their birthday parties. Cutting in from the open top of a grocery carton, make three different sized holes in one side of the box. Cut one hole just a bit bigger than a tennis ball, the next hole two inches bigger than a tennis ball, and the last hole twice the size of a tennis ball, as shown in Figure 8. If you have very

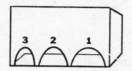

young children you might want to make the holes even larger.

Place the box upside down on the floor. Mark a starting line from 5 to 10 feet away from the box, depending on the age of your children. Some families might want to stagger the starting line, with the younger children starting closer and the older children and parents starting farther back.

Each family member, in turn, tries to roll the ball through one of the holes. The smallest hole counts three points, the next two points, and the largest hole one point. The person with the most points wins.

3. *Hide-and-seek.* This is one of the oldest and most popular games with children. Dads, play this once a week with your small children and you will be sure to win the Best Dad on the Block award. Choose a base and have your child hide. Count to 20 out loud and yell, "Here I come ready or not." If you find him before he touches base, then he is It and must count while you hide. When our children were small, we just took turns hiding.

4. *Balloon fun.* It's amazing how many ways you can use the plain old balloon to have fun. If you always keep a package of balloons around, family fun will be at your fingertips. Here are some ways to use a balloon:

• Keep it floating. For very young children this will be difficult but fun. Keep batting the balloon in the air; don't let it hit the floor.

• Volleyball. Tape or in some way attach a string across a room in your house. Choose teams for balloon volleyball.

Score like regular volleyball. Give the small children a chance to hit the ball. Remember that competition within the family should never take the place of being considerate of one another. Allowances always need to be made for younger children.

• Balloon tag. Choose someone to be It. He must chase other family members around as he hits the balloon. When he is able to hit the balloon so it touches another family member, then that person is It.

• Balloon football. We play this in our hallway and the children love it. The football field can be a hall or a room. Divide the family into two equal teams. The idea of the game is for one team to bat the balloon in the air over the other team's goal line without the balloon hitting the floor. The defense tries to hit the balloon downward so it will hit the floor. If the balloon hits the floor, the opposing team takes over and tries to hit the ball over the opposite goal line.

To start the game, one team kicks off (hits the balloon toward the other team). The receiving team hits the balloon until it scores a touchdown or the ball hits the floor. Better set a time limit on this game. It can get rough.

• Balloon soccer. Play balloon soccer like regular soccer. Simply set two goals and have teams try to kick the balloon over the opposing team's goal. Have plenty of spare balloons ready.

5. *Ring toss.* Give each family member a two-foot section of aluminum foil from which to make a ring. First roll the foil into a straight piece, and then form a ring by twisting the two ends together.

Next, find three pop bottles and place them, one in front of the other, about a foot apart. These are the targets for the rings. If a family member tosses his ring around the bottle nearest the starting line, he scores one point. If he encircles the second, he gets three points and if he circles the last bottle he gets five points. The first person to score 20 points is the winner. Your starting line should be from five to ten feet away from the bottles; decide what distance is best for your family.

Another type of target is a chair turned upside-down. Assign a point total to each leg. Family members toss their rings over the legs of the chair.

6. *Holf*. What is Holf? Why, house golf, of course. Mothers, I'm sure you will be delighted to know you can turn your house into a miniature golf course.

Each room, except the bathrooms, will be a hole. If you have seven usable rooms then you will have a seven-hole holf course. Cut two-foot sections of string for each room you are going to use. Tie the ends of each section of string together. Place one of these string circles on the floor in each room. Number your rooms.

A tennis ball will serve as your holf ball. Each person will need a Holf Club. Great flexibility can be used here as family members find something with which they can hit the ball. It can be a yardstick, ruler, plain old stick from a tree, umbrella, broom handle, etc.

Assign a par of four for each hole. Each person should keep his own score on an index card. Starting with hole one, each person gets one hit, in turn, until he gets his ball in the "hole." He then marks down how many hits it took him. When each person has completed the "hole," the family moves on to the next "hole" using the same procedure until all have been played. Players total up scores and the family member with the smallest score wins.

Be as creative as you wish with your Holf Course, and how you play the game. You may want to place obstacles in the way of the holes, assign different pars, or make larger or smaller circles.

7. *Paper plane aerobatics*. Remember the good old days when children used to make paper planes? This activity seems to have flown out the window and has been replaced with our modern, space-age inventions such as television. But old-fashioned activities, such as paper airplanes, when made as a family project, can be great fun. Here are some examples of

what your family can do together on Paper Plane Aerobatics Day.

Each person makes a paper airplane. The little children might need help from the older more experienced pilots. Each person should have time to test his plane to make sure it is ready for the contest. Here are some events to include in your contest.

• Blind landing. Place a target such as a rock or stick if you are outside or a pillow or plate if you are inside. Each person, in turn, is blindfolded, and tries to see how close he can land his airplane to the target. Now try this with the blindfolds off.

• Airborne record. Have each family member fly his airplane to see which one can stay in the air the longest.

• Upside-down flight. Have each person fly his airplane upside-down and see which one can go the farthest.

• Tight squeeze. For this flight, have each family member line up at the end of a hall. The idea is to fly the airplane down the hall without it touching either side. Place a pillow at the end of the hall for the landing strip. If the airplane goes down the hall without touching the sides, the pilot scores two points. If it also hits the landing strip, he scores another three points. Give each person five flights.

• Airplane catch. Divide your family into pairs and have the pairs line up 10-15 feet apart, facing one another. At a given signal, each person is to fly his plane toward the other person who is to try to catch the plane. For eye safety, use only blunt-nose models for this game.

8. *Freeze tag.* Appoint one family member to be It. He chases the other family members until he is able to tag someone. That person must "freeze" in the exact position he was tagged. Other family members should try to "unfreeze" him by touching him. The game is over when all family members have been frozen or It gives up.

9. *Did It Happen?* Write the following statements on 10 separate slips of paper.

a. My most embarrassing moment
b. The best thing I ever did
c. The most interesting person I ever met
d. The worst day I can remember
e. The best day I can remember
f. The funniest thing that has ever happened to me
g. The time I was most afraid
h. My greatest accomplishment
i. The funniest thing I have ever seen someone else do
j. The dumbest thing I have ever done

Fold the slips of paper and put them in a bowl. Each family member draws out a slip until all slips have been drawn. Explain that family members must tell a story based on the slip they drew. This story may be true or false. While the story is being told, if a family member feels the story is false, he may "gong" (hit the lids of two pans together) that person. The person then stops his story and tells whether the story was true or false.

If the story was false, the person who "gonged" may ask the storyteller to do a consequence (like run around the house, stand on his head, etc.). If the storyteller says his story was true (and the rest of the family agree that it was), then he may ask the "gonger" to do a consequence.

This procedure continues until all the statements have been used.

10. Penny toss. Are you ready to spend some money? If so, this game could be a winner for you. Place a large calendar, (at least 6" x 9"), at one end of your table. Give each person one penny. Explain that the object of the game is to toss the penny onto one of the days of the month. The higher the number, the greater reward. For example, if a person throws his penny and it lands on the 21, he will get 21 pennies. If the penny lands on a line, there is no score. Each family member gets 10 throws.

Now, if this seems a little expensive to you, use some other good options. Instead of pennies, use peanuts or M & Ms. Or you can just keep score and name as the winner the person who scored the most points.

11. Paper race. Give each family member two large sheets of paper. Determine a starting and finish line. Each family member is to race toward the finish line but may only step on the paper, moving ahead one step at a time. At no time may a contestant's foot touch the ground, or he is disqualified.

12. Pillow fight. This is an ancient family tradition that always proves to be a painful delight. Sometimes I will announce that we are going to have a pillow fight, and other times the idea arises spontaneously in our family. Each person gets a fluffy pillow and tries to hit another family member with it. Warning: pillows can hurt if swung hard. The family must understand that this is just for fun and that pillows should not be swung hard at another's head. A family member who violates this rule must sit out the rest of the fight. Call time when you have had enough.

13. Table ball roll. You need four players (if there are more than four in your family you can team up) and two tennis balls. Position one team at the ends of the table and the other teams on the sides. The team at the ends of the table tries to roll the ball the length of the table. The opposing team on the side tries to prevent this by rolling their ball across the table to strike the other ball. Score one point for the team that is able to roll the ball the length of the table. Score 3 points for each time a team knocks the opponent's ball off the table. Each team gets 10 turns at trying to roll the ball the length of the table. Alternate positions.

14. Table pool. Tape a styrofoam cup at each corner of one end of your table. Tape another cup an equal distance between the two cups. The top of the cups should be even with the top of your table. You will need a Ping-Pong ball and a pencil. Each person, in turn, hits the Ping-Pong ball with his pencil, as if playing pool. The object is to get the Ping-Pong ball into one of the cups. The cup on the left scores one point, the cup in the middle three points, and the cup on the right five points. Each family member gets 10 shots.

15. Follow the leader. The little ones will especially like this game. One person is appointed leader. The rest of the family must do exactly as the leader does. It is best to have a set amount of time for a person to be It. Each family member should get a turn at being the leader.

16. Plus and minus. This game can be played inside or outside. You will need a two-foot square marked off in nine eight-inch sections, as shown in Figure 9. You can draw this

on the sidewalk or use a large piece of cloth, or butcher paper.

Number the sections 1-9. Find two flat jar caps or cut out similar-size cardboard discs; just about any small round disc will do. Write plus on one and minus on the other.

Mark a starting line three to five feet from the game board. Each person tosses the two discs. All numbers where the plus disc lands are added to the score and all numbers where the minus disc lands are subtracted from the score. If the disc does not land on the game board, the person deducts five from his score. Each person should get 10 turns. The highest total wins.

17. Hang tag. This is a very strenuous form of tag, and also a lot of fun. When a person is hanging by his hands from something (such as a tree), he cannot be tagged. Whenever his feet hit the ground he can be tagged. This is a good form of tag to play at a park where there are lots of monkey bars or trees with low-hanging branches.

18. Favorites-in-rows. Each person makes his own game board of 16 squares from a regular-size sheet of paper. Here's an easy way to do it: have each family member fold his paper from left to right two times lengthwise. You will now have a long narrow strip of paper. Fold this strip in half from top to bottom two times. Open the paper and you will have your game board of 16 squares.

The game is played like bingo. Each family member, in turn, gives a favorite such as horse, candy, vacation, etc. When the word is given each person writes that word in any one of his 16 squares. After 16 favorites have been given, the leader reads back the words from his own paper, going from left to right.

As the leader reads a word, each family member puts a large X in the appropriate square. The person who gets four squares in a row, diagonally, vertically, or horizontally is the winner. Play this game as many times as you wish, perhaps changing categories each time, with the winner being the leader for the next game.

19. Predictions. Each family member, including Mom and Dad, will get to be the center of attraction in this game. Choose who will go first and have him sit in the middle of the room. Each family member, in turn, must make predictions about what that person will be doing 10 years from now. Predictions should include: job, family, accomplishments, etc.

20. Object tag. An object such as a ball, stick, etc. is chosen for this game. The person who is It must touch the person who has the object and then that person is It. The object can be passed by handing it to another person who cannot refuse to take it.

21. Call catch. Have the family stand in a small circle. One person tosses the ball into the air and yells out the name of another family member. The person named must then catch the ball. If he misses, he becomes It and must toss up the ball. If you have smaller children, the person tossing the ball should call out their names occasionally and let them have an "easy catch."

22. Shoe kick. Do you have a big backyard and some old shoes? If so, then you will be able to manage this game. Mark a starting line. Each person loosens up one of his shoes (or puts on an old one) and sees how far he can kick it. Measure distances and name the winner "shoe kicker of the year."

23. Predicaments. One person leaves the room and the rest of the family decides on a predicament. For example, "lost on a desert island." The person returns and tries to find out what kind of predicament he is in by asking family members, "What would you do?" The person must answer thinking of what he would do in that predicament. When It discovers his predicament, let another family member leave the room, and repeat the procedure.

24. Mimic the masters. Have one person leave the room. Decide which of the remaining family members will be the Master. The Master leads the family in weird actions such as stomping his foot, sticking out his tongue, or scratching his stomach. The person who is It must discover who the Master is by watching closely when the actions are changed. The family should sit in a circle while It stands in the middle, watching closely to catch the Master. Let each family member have a turn being the Master and being It.

9
Homemade Holidays

"Our favorite family Christmas tradition," a father once told me, "is a Christmas card project. We do two things. First we read each day's Christmas cards at the evening meal. Each person reads a card and then prays for the person who sent it. Then, when we have received the last cards, we have a Christmas card contest."

"A Christmas card contest?" I asked. "How do you do that?"

"We lay all the cards out on a table. Then we choose (1) the message that best describes the meaning of Christmas, (2) the best picture on a Christmas card, (3) the cutest Christmas card and (4) the Christmas card we were most surprised to receive."

"We then design a small "thank-you" award card to send to the winners of our Christmas card contest. It gets to be quite a big deal with our friends to see who is going to receive an award each year."

"Wow! What a great idea," I thought. "Our family will have to try a Christmas card contest this year." And we did. In fact, it has become one of our favorite Christmas family traditions.

Traditions, those activities that we do year after year, are what homemade holidays are all about. They are great sources of family unity. Some traditions are handed down from generation to generation. Others, we create ourselves. Still others we learn from friends and make our own, such as my family did with the Christmas card contest.

Over a period of years we build traditions that give our children a real sense of family togetherness and security. In this "Homemade Holiday Idea Chapter," there are activities that you might want to adopt as family traditions, or perhaps just use once to enrich your family time together.

The activities center around Easter, Christmas, and Thanksgiving, the major holidays celebrated in most families.

Christmas Family Activity Ideas

"Christmas sometimes seems to be such a hassle," a mother once confided in me. "With all the emphasis on buying presents, and on Santa Claus, I sometimes wish there wasn't such a time of year. And then I feel guilty because I know we should be happily celebrating Jesus' birth."

Do you ever feel this way? I'm sure most parents have, at one time or another. I really believe that Christmas does not have to be a hassle. But the key is planning. We can plan to make Christmas a real family time—a time to do creative activities that will focus on the birth of Christ.

I suggest that you sit down with your spouse sometime during November, or earlier, and decide what you want your Christmas to be like this year. Janet and I do this each year, and it works well. We decide on gifts and then we plan activities that the family will do together. We complete our shopping for presents by December first so that we can concentrate on more important things during December.

Here are some activities that can help make your Christmas a family time that focuses on Jesus.

Advent Wreath
One of our family's favorite traditions is the Advent Wreath.

An Advent Wreath is an arrangement of styrofoam, ever-greens, and candles that provides a colorful setting for the family's Christmas devotions or family nights.

To make an Advent Wreath you will need a round styro-foam base—about 12 inches in diameter and at least one inch thick; floral clay; four red or lavender 8" candles; one white 10" candle; greens from a tree or artificial Christmas greens. Use a table knife to cut five triangular holes in the styrofoam base. Make each hole a bit smaller than the base of the candles. The white candle goes in the center, and the colored candles are evenly spaced around the outside edge of the styrofoam circle. Insert each candle by wrapping its base with a bit of floral clay and pushing it straight down into the hole. Cover the base with greenery. Use long straight pins to hold the greenery in place.

The four red or lavender candles represent the years of waiting for the Messiah. The white center candle represents Christmas Day. On each Sunday in Advent you will light a new candle as the family gathers around to read Scripture, think about the events surrounding the birth of Christ, and to pray together.

Depending on your ethnic background and liturgical tra-dition, you may be familiar with other color combinations for the candles, and themes for other devotions.

Week 1. Light the first candle which represents the proph-ets. Read Isaiah 9:6; 40:3-11; Micah 5:2; Jeremiah 23:5-6. Discuss these Scriptures and the way they were fulfilled in the birth of Christ.

Week 2. Light the first and second candles. The second one represents John the Baptist. Read Malachi 3:1-3; Luke 1:5-22, 57-80. Discuss why God prepared the people for the coming of His Son with someone like John the Baptist and why we need to prepare ourselves for the celebration of His coming.

Week 3. Light the first, second, and third candles. The third one represents Mary and Joseph. Read Luke 1:26-35,

46-55; Matt. 1:18-25. Discuss how Mary felt when she first heard that she was to be the mother of Jesus, Mary's song of praise, and how you feel about the birth of Jesus.

Week 4. Light the first, second, third, and fourth candles. Read Luke 2:1-20. The fourth candle represents the shepherds. Discuss how they must have felt when the birth of Jesus was announced by the angels. Play Christmas charades. A charade is any game in which one or more players act out a title, slogan, name or proverb for the other players to guess.

One family member thinks of a scene from the Christmas story and acts it out for others to guess. Usually the player who guesses correctly is the one to act out the next charade. Examples of scenes that could be acted out are: wise men and the star, shepherds in the field, Jesus in the manger, shepherds visiting Jesus.

Christmas Day. Light all the candles. The center candle represents Christ. Read Luke 2:1-20 again, this time letting your children pantomime while you read it aloud. Even young children can pantomime. You might want to use simple costumes.

Other Christmas Activities

1. Christmas word game. Give each family member pencil and paper. Allow five minutes for them to form as many words as possible from the letters in the word "Christmas." At the end of this activity see who has the most.

2. A Christmas game—20 questions. Each member of your family in turn will think of something in the Christmas story, either person, place or thing. Choose one person to go first. That person says his word's category while the rest of the family tries to discover his word by asking not more than 20 yes-or-no questions. Ask questions from left to right so each person has a chance to quiz the "thinker."

3. Cookie calling night. Christmas is a time to think of others. Save one night to make cookies to take to shut-ins in your church or a nursing home. Even the very young children can participate in this. They will never forget the joy of seeing older persons express happiness as they receive the cookies and special attention.

4. *Jesus acrostic.* Have each person letter "Jesus" vertically on a piece of paper in acrostic fashion as shown. Explain that everyone is to think of words associated with Jesus that start with each of the letters. Have each person read his words. Discuss what these words have to say about Jesus. For example:

> J —Joy
> E—Eternal
> S—Son
> U—Unity
> S—Saviour

5. *Special ornaments.* One of our traditions is to buy a special ornament by which to remember each Christmas. We talk about each ornament at Christmastime and see if we can remember highlights of that Christmas.

6. *Bake a "Jesus Birthday Cake."* This works especially well with a young child. Have a birthday party for Jesus with cake and all. Let your child help you make the cake. Put one candle on it to represent Jesus. Your child might have some ideas on how to decorate the cake. This will help your child remember that the real reason for Christmas is to celebrate Jesus' birth.

7. *Surprise Advent Calendar.* This is our children's all-time favorite Christmas activity. And it's easy to see why. We have a piece of poster-board with pockets (small envelopes cut in half) pasted on it. The pockets are numbered from the first day of December to Christmas Day, as shown in Figure 10.

In each of the pockets we place a slip of paper with a special surprise written on it. Starting with the first day of December, each evening at dinner one of the girls gets to draw out a slip and read what the surprise will be for that evening. This is also a good time to read a verse of Scripture that tells part of the Christmas story.

```
start here
 25   24   23   22   21   20

 19   18   17   16   15   14

 13   12   11   10    9    8

  7    6    5    4    3    2

  1
```

Here are some of the things we have written on the slips of paper:

 • Look under your pillow and you will find a candy bar.
 • Tonight we will go downtown and look at the store windows.
 • Under your bed you will find something to be read. (A book)
 • We will listen to our new Christmas record.
 • Tonight we will drive around the town looking at Christmas lights.
 • Let's make Christmas candy.
 • Invite over the family of your choice for dessert.
 • Light a fire and read together—special dessert.

We include lots of little surprises that we pick up during the year. This becomes a real challenge to come up with different things each year. Our children's enthusiastic response, however, makes the effort worthwhile.

Easter Family Activity Ideas

On Easter Day, two years ago, our family was worshiping in a small church in Washington State. During the service a young man was sitting next to our youngest daughter, Bridget, then age five. The pastor made a comment about Easter that this young man felt needed clarification for Bridget. He said a few words to Bridget, and she proceeded to fill the young man in on the details he had left out.

The man, with a surprised look on his face, leaned over and commented to me, "She sure knows a lot about Easter, doesn't she?"

I was very amused at the scene, but not really surprised, because Bridget was merely passing on information she had learned as a result of a family Easter project.

For four family nights preceding Easter, our family had worked together making a frieze (a series of pictures that tell a complete story) on the last week of Christ's life on earth. We had taken a large roll of butcher paper, rolled it out on the floor, and marked off five 2′ x 2′ sections. On each of the four nights, we drew a picture of a significant event about the Easter story.

The first week we drew a picture of the Triumphal Entry (John 12:12-29). The second week we drew the Last Supper (Luke 22:1-23). The third week we drew a picture of the trial (Mark 15:1-15). The fourth week we drew a picture of the Crucifixion (Mark 15:16-47). Then Easter Sunday we completed our frieze by drawing a picture of the Resurrection.

We would first read and discuss the Scripture of the evening. We then decided what we would draw and assigned family members various parts of the picture. During the week the frieze was hung on the dining room wall. This family project really helped our whole family deepen its understanding of the death and resurrection of Christ.

Doing things together during Easter season can help reduce the effects of commercialism on your family. Doing creative biblical Easter family activities is far more effective than trying to do away with the Easter bunny, Easter egg hunts, or new clothes. With proper positive emphasis on the true meaning of Easter in your family, these other "commercial" aspects of Easter will take a less dominant role.

Plan now what activities you would like your family to do together during the Easter season. Here are some ideas you might want to try with your family. Be creative. Feel free to try activities that aren't listed in this book.

Easter Activities

1. Create an Easter frieze. This is already explained in the preceding section. Be sure to start early on this project as it may take several weeks to complete.

2. Have a Family Lord's Supper. This would be a good opportunity to explain to your children some of the deep meanings of the Lord's Supper (Luke 22:1-23).

3. Feelings of Easter. Read Mark 15:16-47 and try to capture some of the feelings surrounding the Crucifixion. Discuss: How do you think Jesus' mother felt? How do you think the soldiers felt? What do you think Jesus' disciples were thinking about? How did they feel? What was the difference in feelings between the two thieves on the cross? How do you feel when you think of the Crucifixion?

4. Publish a family newspaper. Read Mark 15—16 as a family and then write a newspaper called the *Jerusalem News.* Try to imagine what might have been written in a newspaper the day after the tomb was found empty. Assign your reporters (family members) short articles on the various aspects of Jesus' death and resurrection. For instance, the headlines might read: "Jesus Reportedly Seen Alive," Family members could report with stories such as "Soldier Reports Body Stolen," "Have Jesus' Prophecies about Himself Come True?" "Soldier at the Cross Reports Strange Happenings," and "Was Jesus the Messiah?" If your family is artistic, you might want to illustrate the *Jerusalem News.*

5. Read together. Last year our family read aloud together *God and a Boy Named Joe,* by Ethel Barrett (Regal). This is an excellent read-aloud book about the last week of Jesus, seen through the eyes of a young Jewish boy.

6. Easter drama. There are many parts of the Easter story that your family can act out together. The Triumphal Entry, the trial, the Resurrection, can all be acted out simply but effectively. Simple costumes and props help. This works well with the younger children.

7. Forgiveness thoughts. Give family members a pencil and

piece of paper and ask them to write *forgiveness* at the top of the paper. Read Luke 23:34. Discuss Jesus' attitude about forgiveness. Next tell family members that you will give them three minutes to write down all their thoughts about forgiveness. These can be Scriptures, feelings, times they have forgiven or not forgiven others, times when they have not been forgiven by someone else, what they want to do.

At the end of the three minutes, have everyone share his thoughts on forgiveness. Share how Christ's forgiveness affects our behavior toward others.

8. *On-the-street interviews.* Your family can have some real fun with this activity. Appoint one family member to be the "on-the-street" television interviewer. The rest of the family can be people who were associated with Jesus in Bethlehem, such as a storekeeper, soldier, tax collector, Pharisee, disciple, cousin, restaurant owner, etc. The man-on-the-street interviews each person, asking such questions as "How long have you known Jesus?" "What did you think of Him? "Do you think He really is the Messiah?" "Do you think He will rise from the dead?"

Each family member being interviewed should try to put himself into the person's shoes and try to answer how he feels that person in Jesus' time would have answered.

When the interviews are done, have a discussion on how the various people felt about Jesus and why they felt that way.

9. *New Life poster.* Give each person a sheet of poster-size paper, marking pens, scissors, glue, and magazines. Explain that each person is to make a New Life poster. A family member can decorate his poster in any way he wishes to depict "new life." He can find pictures that show new life, draw a picture or symbols.

Share your posters and discuss: How does Easter symbolize new life? How does the Resurrection guarantee us new life today? How does this affect the way we live?

10. *Color Easter Eggs.* You probably already do this, but why not add a special feature this year? Have your children

decorate one egg with a thought about Jesus. They can do this easily with marking pens. Have family members "show-and-tell" their eggs. Thank God for His great gift, Jesus.

Thanksgiving Family Activity Ideas

Thanksgiving is possibly our greatest North American holiday for family togetherness. Perhaps this is why the U.S. President has designated the week of Thanksgiving "National Family Week." Include with your festivities this year some times centered around God's Word, as well as creative family activities.

Thanksgiving Activities

1. T Stands for Thankful. Make a large block *T* out of butcher paper or poster board and tape it to a wall in your home. Give family members magazines and have them cut out pictures or words that represent things for which they are thankful. (You may draw the pictures if you prefer.) Work together as a family and paste these pictures on the *T*. When the *T* has been completely covered, ask each person why he is thankful for the items he chose. Read Ephesians 5:20. Discuss: Why does God want us to give thanks to Him? In what ways are we especially blessed in North America? Take a family vote and select the one item on the *T* for which the family is most thankful.

2. Thanksgiving add-a-word. This is a good activity to do at the dinner table. Have one family member think of something for which he is thankful and say it aloud. The next person thinks of something for which he is thankful that starts with the last letter of the word just said. For example, if the person said *food*, the next person would say *dad* which begins with *d*, the last letter in the word *food*. Go around the family circle as many times as you like with each person adding a word. Read Philippians 4:6. Talk about why people worry about things. How does this verse say we should present our needs to God?

3. Thankful for Indians. Tell your children the story of the first American Thanksgiving. Mention that the Pilgrims were thankful for Squanto and Samoset, two Indians who showed them how to plant corn. Tell your children that you are going to teach them to play an Indian children's game.

Get a straight stick about a foot long and attach a heavy piece of twine about 14 inches long. Punch a small hole in the bottom of a paper cup. Put the string through this hole and tie a knot on the inside of the cup. Try to catch the cup on the end of the stick.

4. *Pin the tail on the turkey*. Draw a large turkey, minus the tail feathers, on a piece of butcher paper or poster board and attach it to the wall. From construction paper cut out a large turkey tail feather for each family member. On the tail feather, have each person draw a picture of something he is thankful for, and then share it with the rest of the family. Blindfold each family member, in turn, and have him pin or tape his tail feather on the turkey.

5. *Make a family Thanksgiving book*. Discuss as a family and decide upon one thing for which you are thankful that starts with each letter in the word Thanksgiving. For example for *T* you might select trees; for *H*, home; for *A*, America, etc. Next, assign each family member several pages of the book to illustrate. Use a separate 8½" by 11" piece of paper for each letter. For example, if the family selected Home to represent the letter *H*, the person illustrating that letter could draw a picture of your home with your family standing in front, or cut out of a magazine a picture that symbolizes the warmth of home.

Allow each family member flexibility in designing his own pages. Select one family member to design the cover. When the project is completed, each person can show his pages.

Talk about the many things for which the family can be thankful. Have a circle of prayer with each person thanking God for specific things He has provided. Staple the pages of the book together or punch holes and tie them with yarn. Display the book throughout the Thanksgiving season.

10
Togetherness Through Work and Hobbies

Two years ago I held a family night seminar in a little wheat town in eastern Washington. Many of the seminar participants in this small town of Pomeroy had teenagers.

It was very unusual to have that many parents with adolescents attending a family night seminar. Even more astounding was that I did not get the usual objections to my family night ideas such as "That will never work with our teenagers," or "We'll never be able to get them together on the same night," or "They just wouldn't be interested."

I mentioned to the pastor that I was surprised at the positive attitude of the parents with teenagers.

"I'm not at all surprised," he replied. "These families work together in the wheat fields and on farms. Children are used to doing things with their parents. Family nights just fit beautifully into the lives of these families."

Working together as a family creates a strong family bond. Togetherness comes naturally as parents interact with children and brothers and sisters interact together.

For many centuries it was necessary for families to work together. Making a living depended on it. Children felt needed. An ancient Chinese proverb says, "A man's wealth is in the number of sons he has."

Things have changed. In our country, children are more of a liability than an economic asset. As you well know, raising a child is expensive. Children rarely feel they are really needed to help at home. This is a shame. Everyone within a family needs to feel he is needed and that he contributes to the success of the home.

Children *can* feel like they are an important part of the family. But it takes vision and planning on the part of parents. We need to find meaningful work for our families to do together. This is not easy. It's much simpler to load the dishwasher, wash the car, vacuum the floor, etc. ourselves than to go through the hassle of supervising our children. I would like to suggest some ways that you can involve your children in family chores and give them a sense of accomplishment.

Even a preschool child can be taught the value of working together as a family. You'll notice that little children (really all children) do not like to work alone. Have you ever noticed the lost look when you tell your child to clean up a room he has just devastated with toys? It's true he made the mess, but what a difference in attitude when he realizes the rest of the family is going to help him with his monumental task. Later you can ask this little worker to help you—perhaps to empty the wastebaskets or dust or help clear the table.

Working Together
As your children get older, plan ways for the family to work together. Here are a few ideas.

1. Yard work. This is a natural. Set aside an hour (or two) a week during the summer for the entire family to work in the yard. Make it fun by telling your children when the work is done you will have a treasure hunt for candy. Send the children inside and hide pieces of wrapped candy around the yard.

2. Wash the car. This can be fun for the family to do together. Even the little ones can slop water on the wheels (and themselves). When you complete the car wash, have a five-minute water fight.

3. Clean the house. We find that an hour or so of hard work on a Saturday can get the house cleaned up and ready for Sunday. The entire family participates. We divide up responsibilities and go at it. Housework is not nearly as painful when you know others in the family are working toward the same goal.

4. Projects for others. You have a great Christian opportunity to work together as a family for others. How about the widows in your church, the elderly or shut-ins? Could they use some help in their yards? What about some difficult cleaning jobs such as washing windows? Your family could work together on a project for the church.

5. Clean the garage. Is this Dad's exclusive job? Why not have the entire family work together with Dad?

6. Paint. This is a good family project for families with older children.

7. Dinner. Here's an exceptional daily opportunity to have the family work together. One person can help with the meal, another set the table and another clean the table and wash the dishes. In our home Janet is not supposed to have anything to do with clean up. She is in charge of the evening meal so the rest of the family cleans up while she does what she wishes.

8. Seasonal cleaning. Every year brings some "big" job that takes special effort. Why not mark one day on the calendar and have the entire family spend the day working around the house. Mom and Dad should organize the work and assign the jobs.

I realize that many times doing some of these things yourself would be easier than involving your children, but remember the long-range benefits. Children who can work with others value work, can work toward and accomplish goals, feel needed and have a sense of family togetherness.

Togetherness Through Hobbies

I knew a Chinese family in San Rafael, California, that spent hours together gardening a small plot of ground. Their children were preschool age but you could see that they already loved this family hobby. The parents were very patient. They allowed the children to plant the seeds. They explained in detail the growth process. This was a shared activity that the family loved. It was a hobby that gave the family a great sense of togetherness.

Hobbies, those activities we do in our leisure hours, have built togetherness in many families over the years. Does your family have a hobby—something you all do together and enjoy? If not, look through the following list of suggested hobbies and see if there is one you would like to start. Talk it over with the family and plan for many hours of enjoyment and family togetherness. Check books out of the library about the hobby you select.

Also:

Coins
Model airplanes
Astronomy
Archery
Costume dolls
Autographs
Bowling
Boating
Mountain climbing
Skating
Stamps
Miniature horses
Flower arranging
Ceramics
Music
Rocks and minerals

Driftwood art
Leathercraft
Horseback riding
Swimming
Skiing
Camping
Pen pals
Puppets
Jogging
Photography
Pets
Magic
Homemade dolls
Carving
Reading

11
Togetherness Through Reading

"Our way of building a spirit of togetherness in our family," Mrs. Kelly said, "is to read together as a family at the dinner table each evening."

Mr. Kelly agreed. "Reading has been good for us. I've been terribly busy at times, but we have always been able to take time to read after our evening meal."

I glanced in the other room where the Kelly children were watching television. The two boys were obviously high school age and the girl in grade school.

"You mean those boys still like to read together as a family at their age?" I asked in disbelief.

"Oh yes," replied Mrs. Kelly. "Things really haven't changed over the years. The boys like this time together as much as ever."

That night before I left the Kelly home Mrs. Kelly handed me a book called *Little House in the Big Woods*. "Maybe you'd like to try reading aloud with your family," she said. "I'd like to share one of our favorite books with you."

That night I told Janet about the idea of reading together and she agreed that it sounded fun. The next evening after dinner I announced to the children that we were going to read a book together—perhaps a chapter or two each evening.

Heidi, then in the third grade said, "That sounds like fun, Dad." Liesl, however, was less than excited.

"I don't like the idea. Why do we have to read?"

"Well Liesl," I replied, "if you really don't want to be a part of this then you may be excused. But don't bother us while we are reading."

Liesl left the table and went to her room while the rest of us read the first chapter of *Little House in the Big Woods*. While I was reading I heard some strange noises in the hall. I was sure it was Liesl listening quietly (for her) just a few feet away.

The next evening when dinner was over Liesl did not ask to leave the table. In fact, guess who howled most for "just one more chapter, please Dad!"

We spent several months reading through the *Little House* series. It was a delightful family adventure all the way.

Eyes were teary when Jack, the Ingall's family dog, was lost when fording a river. We bit our nails when some unfriendly Indians walked into the Ingall's home while Pa was away. We could almost feel the despair when Pa's crops failed once again, leaving the family terribly poor. Of course, Nellie Oleson was unforgettable. We had real sadness in our family when we read about Mary's blindness but were uplifted by Mary's courage and Laura's love as she "became Mary's eyes."

Reading this series of books together brought our close family even closer. When our family reads together, we feel a certain closeness that is hard to explain. The outcome is a real sense of security and family togetherness.

I'm sure by this time you know I am sold on reading together as a family. I can't think of a better way to create a sense of togetherness in a family.

Over the last four years our family has read dozens of books together. We have read a wide variety of books. Some have been Christian books such as Paul White's *Jungle Doctor* series. Others have been mysteries. Some we have enjoyed more than others. But the one thing that never changes is that we enjoy that time together. It is a tradition with deep meaning.

Gladys Hunt in her delightful book on reading, *Honey for a Child's Heart,* shares so well the benefits of a family reading together.

"If families don't read books together, how do they know each other's friends?"

"Reading aloud as a family has bound us together, as sharing in adventure always does. We *do* know the same people. We have gone through emotional crises together as we felt anger, sadness, fear, gladness, and tenderness in the world of the book we are reading. Something happens to us which is better experienced than described—a kind of enlarging of heart—when we encounter passages full of grand language and nobility of thought" (Grand Rapids: Zondervan Publishing House, 1969, p. 75).

A few months ago we ended what was probably our greatest family adventure ever by viewing *The Last Battle.* No, this was not something we watched on TV or at a theater. We viewed this *Last Battle* in our imaginations as we read the last book in C. S. Lewis' *Chronicles of Narnia.* But to go with the excitement of *The Last Battle,* our entire family felt a real sadness. We had just completed the last of this delightful series. Our family adventure was over and somehow we all felt that there could never be another adventure quite like this.

I suggest you buy this series of books for family reading. For children (and adults) first grade and above they are hard to top. Not only are the "Chronicles of Narnia" some of the best children's fiction ever written but they also are based on deep Christian principles and thoughts that surface in surprising ways as you read together.

It was rewarding to watch Heidi's face light up as she discovered that Aslan, the Lion in *The Lion, the Witch and the Wardrobe* was "just like Jesus."

After reading *The Last Battle* our family discussed heaven. "I want to go to heaven," Bridget said.

"You will some day," I replied.

"No Dad, I mean right now. It's better than here."

I guess we all felt like that after reading C. S. Lewis' imaginative description of what heaven is like. Heaven had never been so real to us before. Now tell me, where can you go on a family adventure and end up in heaven and still have your earthly bodies? And for the price of a paperback book!

Are you ready to start a tradition of reading together as a family? If so, then a book that I have already mentioned, *Honey for a Child's Heart,* is a must. This book is all about the imaginative use of books in family life written by a committed Christian. Besides being delightful reading you will find an extensive bibliography of books to use with your family. Mrs. Hunt gives three classifications of books, general, Christian, and family teaching. You will find among her recommendations many books you will be able to use.

Start collecting books to read together as a family. Look closely at the order blanks your children bring home advertising Scholastic books. These are very reasonably priced and usually have good selections that you can read together as a family. Many times we will let our girls order a couple of Scholastic books for themselves and then we will order some to keep on hand for family reading.

Watch for opportunities to pick up good used books at garage sales and secondhand shops. We have found dozens of good books this way. And of course there is always the cheapest and most extensive source of all, your local library.

A few suggestions of books to get you started are listed below. Be sure to preview any book you decide to purchase or borrow to see if you feel your family will enjoy it.

Books for Family Reading

Books for Young Children (ages 0-8)

Heidi by Johanna Spyri

The Story of Ferdinand by Munro Leaf

Mary Poppins by Pamela Travers

The Happy Orpheline by Natalie Savage Carlson
A Brother for the Orphelines by Natalie Savage Carlson
Flicka, Ricka, Dicka (series) by Maj Lindman
Snip, Snapp, Snurr (10 in series) by Maj Lindman
The Tale of Peter Rabbit by Beatrix Potter

Books for Older Children (ages 9-12)
Little House Books (9 in series) by Laura Ingalls Wilder
Chronicles of Narnia (7 in series) by C. S. Lewis
The Borrowers (4 in series) by Nancy Norton
Charlotte's Web by E. B. White
Pippi Longstocking (series) by Astrid Lindgren
The Black Stallion (series) by Walter Farley
Old Bones, the Wonder Horse by Mildred Mastin Pace
All of a Kind Family (3 in series) by Sydney Taylor
The Adventures of Huckleberry Finn by Mark Twain
The Adventures of Tom Sawyer by Mark Twain
Johnny Tremain by Esther Forbes
Little Women by Louisa May Alcott
Justin Morgan Had a Horse by Marguerite Henry
Island of the Blue Dolphins by Scott O'Dell
Voyages of Dr. Dolittle by Hugh Lofting
Call It Courage by Armstrong Sperry
Helen Keller by Stewart and Polly A. Groff
The Family Under the Bridge by Natalie Carlson
Christmas Carol by Charles Dickens
Strawberry Girl by Lois Lenski
Jungle Doctor (series of 4) by Paul White
Arch Books (Concordia)
Hans Brinker by Mary M. Dodge

Books written in the 1600s, 1700s, and 1800s
Pilgrim's Progress by John Bunyan
Gulliver's Travels by Jonathan Swift
Robinson Crusoe by Daniel Defoe
The Swiss Family Robinson by Johann David Wyss
Treasure Island by Robert Louis Stevenson

12

How to Plan for
Family Fun and Togetherness

How many times have you asked yourself, "Where has the summer gone? We've blown it again. We just haven't done the things we talked about doing together as a family."

Janet and I have faced this dilemma and found what we feel to be a workable solution. True, our family activities never seem to measure up completely to our expectations— but we come closer. We feel comfortable with what is happening. I feel this can happen in any family.

The key is planning. "So what's new?" you say. "We already know that. It's just that we never get around to doing it."

You know the problem; then let me suggest a plan of action. Be sure that you and your spouse have both read this book. Now go back over the book individually and put your initial by all the ideas and activities you like and feel the family will enjoy. Next set a time for both of you to plan for family activities. Perhaps you could do this in the evening after the children have gone to bed. Don't get lazy and neglect your scheduled planning meetings. You will need a planning calendar, and can usually buy these at a book or variety store.

Don't try to cover too much ground on this first planning session. In fact, a goal could be to plan one new thing to do together as a family during the following month. Don't become overly ambitious and set goals too high to achieve. It's best to do one thing well and then move on to the next.

Here are some discussion questions and planning procedures for each chapter. Look through these and choose the *one* that is most interesting to you right now; the one that your family needs most. Plan in that area.

Chapter 1. *Family Fun and Togetherness—Who Needs It?* Do we need more quality family time, or are we satisfied with what we are currently doing?

Chapter 2. *Family Night—Best Night of the Week.* Are family nights something that could build our family? Is this something we want to do? (Make a decision.) What night would be best for family night? Mark this on your calendar. Don't let anything interfere! What will we do on our first family night? Plan in detail. You might need to purchase some of the resources mentioned in the chapter or use one of the family night plans.

Chapter 3. *Togetherness Around the Table.* Are we satisfied with our mealtimes? How could they be improved? Would we like to do some activities listed in this chapter? Which ones? When will we do them? (Mark these on your planning calendar.)

Chapter 4. *Trips, Vacations, and Other Great Adventures.* Are any trips or vacations coming up? If so, what principles in this chapter could help make our trip or vacation more enjoyable? Write down some of the specific things you are going to do on this trip.

Chapter 5. *Celebrations of Special and Not-so-special Occasions.* Choose one activity out of this chapter that you would like to do with your family. Mark it on the calendar even if it is long range.

Chapter 6. *Family Activities That Say "I Care."* Is this an area in which our family needs to improve? What activities would encourage caring and building self-esteem in our family? Plan for at least one of the activities. Mark it on the calendar.

Chapter 7. *Three Games to Make and Play.* Which of the three games would best suit the needs of our family? Should parents make this game or should the entire family make it together? If you have time, make the game now. If not, mark on your calendar when you will make it, and when you will play it with your family.

Chapter 8. *Simple Games for Family Fun.* Review the activities in this chapter that you initialed. What ones did you both initial? Write two activities on your calendar that you will do during the next month.

Chapter 9. *Homemade Holidays.* Is a holiday coming up soon? If so, plan for that holiday. Decide when you will do the various activities you choose. Do you have enough of a spiritual emphasis?

Chapter 10. *Togetherness Through Work and Hobbies.* Do you use work as a means of family togetherness? Plan a work project to do as a family. Write the date on the calendar. Are you interested in starting a family hobby? Set aside a time when you can discuss this with your family.

Chapter 11. *Togetherness Through Reading.* Is this something you would like your family to do? If so, choose a book right now that you think your family will enjoy. Decide who will purchase or borrow the book. On your calendar mark a date when you will start reading it.

Now, I have just shared with you Janet's and my approach to planning for family activities. I'm sure, as you read through these planning suggestions and decide on which one you would key on first, that you realized one planning session is not enough. You're right. Janet and I plan weekly. Sometime during the week we sit down with the calendar and make family decisions. Now, of course, all this time is not spent planning family activities. Sometimes it takes quite a while just to get our personal schedules straight. We do usually plan for family night during this time.

Our weekly planning time is one of the best things that has ever happened to our marriage. Before we started this we had frequent misunderstandings about schedules. Now those conflicts are almost nonexistent. Besides planning for family activities, we feel we can communicate about anything during this time. Major decisions (and of course minor ones too), problems with the children, and a host of other things are discussed. We always end the time by reading a section of Scripture together, praying for each other, and for the rest of the family.

We have shared this approach to planning and sharing with other couples who have also enriched their marriages in this way. Give it some thought. Discuss it with your spouse. Perhaps it will work for you also.